Who Killed Georgette Bauerdorf?

Pete Diven

Published by Trellis Publishing, 2021.

WHO KILLED GEORGETTE BAUERDORF?

First edition. July 14, 2021.

Copyright © 2021 Pete Diven.

ISBN: 979-8224901029

Written by Pete Diven.

WHO KILLED GEORGETTE BAUERDORF?

PETE DIVEN

A Tragic Heiress

1944 is a world away. We view it through the technicolor Imagery of Saving Private Ryan, or the romance of From Here to Eternity, the heroics of The Longest Day. The truth is more mundane, but no less terrifying for all of that. In Los Angeles men strolled through the city, dressed ready for death and duty. Soon they would board ships to carry them to the theatres of the Pacific. Many knew that they would not return. A strange price to pay for a war that started in Europe and in which Americans had been promised they would not become involved.

It seems strange that the film industry continued in that time of global crisis; but it did, and many stars of Hollywood did their bit for morale, not just in making their films or posing as pin ups for far flung servicemen to drool over. They offered their time to enable the nervous soldiers about to depart for foreign fields to enjoy their short spell on leave a little more.

One of the best attractions for those soldiers and service personnel was the Hollywood Canteen. This was the brain child of Jules Stein, the president of the Music Corporation of America, and the actors Bette Davis and John Garfield. It opened in 1942 and ran until Thanksgiving Day in 1945. Over three thousand actors, directors, producers, cameramen, make-up artists and others connected with Hollywood volunteered to staff this bolt hole for servicemen and women of all allied countries. Although open to all, it was mainly American soldiers, sailors and air force men who frequented the Cahuenga Boulevard restaurant and dance hall. There, the chance was always present that your food would be served by a star of the golden screen, or there would be three minutes of escapism in the arms of a household name during the last dance of the night. Betty Davis delivering your burger, Marlene Dietrich with your meatloaf.

Nearby, the Guild – designed along similar lines - offered a free bed for the night. The only entrance fee for either being your uniform;

but the food was expensive – the cost of a meal your service for your country.

The Canteen was supported by the film industry – stars gave their time freely. In fact, not only the rich and famous worked as volunteers there. The rich and less well known also offered their evenings. Among them was the twenty year old daughter of an oil mogul. Georgette Bauerdorf might not have been a recognisable face in the Canteen, but she was certainly up there with the wealthiest of the Hollywood stars who served the servicemen.

And although her looks might not have been of the sculptured beauty so beloved of the screen, nevertheless, she was a very attractive, welcoming person. Once food was served, the unpaid 'waitresses' would head to the dance floor. There they would waltz and jitterbug with the young soldiers, sailors and flyers soon to find themselves in a far more hostile environment.

For Georgette, it was the slower dances she favoured. The heiress had been born in New York, on May 6th 1924. Her mother had died back in 1935 when Georgette was still a young girl. Father George was a Wall Street Financier, who also held interests in Louisiana, Texas and Nevada. His work kept him away for much of the time, and Georgette was enrolled in the prestigious Marlborough School. The girls there were known as 'Violets'; it was that kind of school. Later she attended the equally well known Westlake School for Girls, which was in the wealthy Holmby Hills section of the city. It was another institute of learning for the children of the rich and famous, among whose alumni were the likes of Shirley Temple. Georgette graduated in 1941. She immediately entered the socialite scene of those early war years.

By 1944, she owned a luxurious apartment in a serviced block. The block provided residents with their own maids, and porterage was always available. Among her neighbours was the actress Virginia Weidler, who was signed up with MGM. Her apartment was sufficiently grand to spread over two floors, and she had her own patio.

Indeed, her home in 'El Palacio' saw her located in one of the more prestigious buildings in Los Angeles.

She drove around in her sister's 1936 coupe, and that would often be left parked outside the block. She really was a girl for whom the future promised so much. But one of the few downsides of living a life where everything is on tap is that such people are not always prepared for the real world. And Los Angeles was an extremely dangerous city. In 1944, most of the soldiers passing through had already seen action. What we know today regarding the likes of post traumatic stress disorder and the emotional damage caused by conflict was not at all understood during the second world war. There were many seriously disturbed young men on the streets of the glamourous city.

Some – perhaps many – of the men passing through Los Angeles were suffering. Their futures were uncertain. A more mature and street wise girl might have put up barriers, looked out for warning signs. Georgette was not that kind of girl. Friends say that she took precautions regarding her safety, but we know she was as happy to dance with and give lifts to strangers just she would with long-time friends.

This was not in anyway to suggest that she was flighty, or flirty – absolutely nothing from the time suggests that these were the case. But she was possessed of an innocence that was down to a sheltered upbringing. She was a good person who saw life positively, and who wanted to offer some of that goodness to others. She did not, it seemed, believe that anybody could be of an opposite disposition.

Still, up to that fateful day in October 1944, life was good. Her best friend was June Ziegler – they had met when Georgette had volunteered to become a junior hostess at the Hollywood Canteen. Georgette also had a day job, working in the Women's Service bureau at the Los Angeles Times. In fact, it turned out that Ziegler also worked there, although in a different department of this large organisation. A third friend, Doris Puckett, joined them at the Hollywood Canteen.

She worked with Ziegler and recalled that their work was not just providing entertainment and a pleasant evening to the servicemen. They would also help with writing letters; many of the men were poorly educated. Georgette may have been extremely privileged, but she was giving back to the community in a meaningful way.

In 1943, she had taken the opportunity provided by her affluent circumstances and chosen to tour the United States. She visited San Francisco then boarded a train to New York – she had not been to her former home for four years. Next it was on to Louisiana, where her father held business interests in the oil industry. But she stayed in touch with June during her tour, sending her post cards and letters. In one, she revealed her enjoyment of the Hollywood Canteen:

'Are you still going to the Canteen? I think of it every Wednesday 'nite even though there seemed to be a majority of jerks there...' she wrote. But the outward worldliness of these words hid the natural innocence she possessed.

That innocence may well have been a factor in the crime that left her raped and strangled to death, which took place in the early hours of one Fall morning.

This innocence was brought home vividly following her death. A soldier got in touch with the investigating officers to tell of an experience he had enjoyed with Georgette. Gordon Aadland was a Sergeant serving on the Aleutian Islands north of the Arctic Circle. While on leave he was staying in Los Angeles with his brother, his family and their mother. On the final night before heading north and back to war once more (the Aleutians were seen as an important strategic outpost which controlled lines of transportation) he took his sister dancing at the Hollywood Palladium. His sister caught the streetcar home, but Aadland needed transport to get back to his brother's house.

He described the incident that followed: 'I needed a ride...No sooner did I get on Sunset and Palisade, motioned with my thumb, than she pulled up in a coupe. She asked, "Where to?" I told her.' In fact, Georgette drove him around for a bit, maybe fifteen minutes, and chatted about her boyfriend and her life.

'She seemed like a friendly girl,' he said 'and I appreciated the ride. But she never should have picked up a soldier around midnight.'

Aadland feared for the safety of this kindly but naïve girl in the uncertain world of a servicemen strewn city during the war. That fear was realised when he read a newspaper report shortly afterwards. He was on the long 3200 mile journey to Alaska when he found a copy of the Los Angeles Times. In it he read the tragic story of the murder of an oil heiress. It seems as though Aadland was the last person, killer apart, to see Georgette alive.

He contacted the police immediately, by letter. But later, on reflection, he wondered if his testimony was helpful to the investigators. He had told them that Georgette had dropped him, and then turned right. But later he realised he had assumed this, and more likely she had continued on down the street, before turning left in the direction of her apartment.

Next he told police that she seemed nervous. She kept looking behind her. But again he wondered later if this was just uncertainty of driving, rather than an attempt to keep an eye open for an unwelcome follower.

Earlier on Wednesday October 11th 1944 Georgette had been out for some shopping and lunch with Rose Gilbert, a friend. 'We shopped and had lunch together,' said Rose. 'She seemed perfectly happy. I was with her until two o'clock in the afternoon.'

At the time, Georgette had a boyfriend, Jerry Brown, who was stationed in Fort Bliss. They had met at the Hollywood Canteen the previous June, and while shopping with Rose she had bought a plane ticket so she could fly to El Paso to see him.

Later, she met another friend, June Weider. June said something that tied in with Aadland's initial thinking. After the crime, she spoke to Deputy Sheriff Hopkinson of the Los Angeles Police Department. '(Georgette) appeared to be nervous,' she said.

Hopkinson added 'She (Georgette) had asked her (June) to spend the evening with her at her apartments. However, she gave no explanation for her nervousness or any reason why she wanted her to spend the night with her.' Later, other friends noticed that the heiress seemed agitated, and not her normal self. However, they put that down to a persistent and rather annoying soldier who insisted that she danced the jitterbug with him. But she preferred waltzes and less frenetic dances.

However, the soldier, Cosmo Volpe, kept cutting in when she was spending time with other servicemen. Later, when suspicions fell on him, he offered a reason for his persistence. 'She was not a good dancer, but wanted to learn,' he said. 'I was a professional dancer back in Astoria, Long Island, and I'm a good jitterbug.' Clearly, although Volpe was initially a person of interest to the police, there was no evidence to connect him to the crime.

After leaving the club at around 11.30pm, Georgette made her way back to her apartment, picking up Aadland on the way. It's believed that she arrived home at about midnight. The janitor of the block heard her walking around her kitchen, her high heels click clacking on the hard floor, at about this time. It seems as though she ate some beans and melon, washed up and threw away the food she had not eaten. Fredrick Atwood believes he heard a tray crashing to the floor shortly after this time. Was it simply something she dropped? Was he in fact mistaken? Or is it possible that an attack had already begun?

Then, at 2.30 am on October 12th another resident of the apartment block heard a woman scream: 'Stop, stop! You're killing me!' But he turned over and went back to sleep, assuming he had been woken by an argument. He did not call the police, or the janitor, or even investigate himself. Who knows, maybe had he done so a homicide would have been prevented. That neighbour must have regretted his decision for the remainder of his days.

The next morning, Attwood, his wife and daughter began their rounds. They were responsible for looking after their wealthy residents, cleaning their apartments for them. But they noticed that the door to Georgette's flat was open. They heard water running, and went inside. They made their way to the bathroom, and there saw Georgette in the bath. She was wearing a pyjama top, but no bottoms. Initially, Attwood thought that she had fallen, and could be saved. He moved her out of the water while his wife turned off the running tap.

But then it was clear that the girl was dead. Her body was bruised; her face cut. She had clearly put up a hard fight. Her stomach was blushed purple, and on her thigh was a handprint complete with the indentations of finger nails piercing her skin. Her knuckles were scraped and smashed. A washing cloth was stuffed into her mouth, so hard and far that it was almost disappeared inside her.

Later, police confirmed that Georgette had been strangled and raped. Nothing was missing from the apartment, including some expensive and visible jewellery. But the light over the entrance to her apartment had been loosened. It was partly unscrewed so that it would not come on. Police concluded that, most likely, the attacker was lying in wait when Georgette returned home. The attack was clearly made with the intent of rape, rather than a burglary that had gone wrong. But the killer, presumably, had taken her car. That was discovered, abandoned, sometime later. There was a dent on the fender, and mechanics deduced that it had been in a collision with another car, but that was never traced. The car was abandoned when it ran out of gas. If the police checked for fingerprints, they did so carelessly, because Aadland knew that his prints were on the passenger side of the car, but police never contacted him to eliminate him from their enquiries.

Captain George Bowers was an officer on the case. A sociable girl working in a gathering spot such as the Hollywood Canteen got to know plenty of men, and over time Bowers put together a short list of suspects to whom he wished to speak. Cosmo Volpe was on that list, but he was not the only person.

A known criminal, Otto Wilson, was linked to the crime, but in a pattern we are about to see develop, that link was tenuous in the extreme. Wilson was a very unpleasant character; a serial rapist and murderer. Some of the violence seen on Georgette's body was typical of his crimes. He was known for mutilating his victims, slashing them with a butcher's knife. There was a psychopathic element to his deeds; he would remove his targets' breasts, or hack away at their vaginas. In the end, Wilson was turned in by his wife, who was becoming increasingly concerned about what she described to police as his bizarre 'sexual impulses'. She told of one occasion when she was undressing to take a shower. Wilson approached her from behind, sliced her bare buttock with a razor and drank the blood that flowed. It was the final cut, and Wilson was turned in. He soon confessed to two murders – but not Georgette's – and was executed within the year. Today, he might expect treatment as well as punishment. A psychiatrist stated, at his trial: 'He was a necrophiliac and cannibalistic, all of which when summed up are the manifestations of the sado-masochistic complex.' Maybe, but he was patently not the killer of Georgette Bauerdorf.

Another name that emerged in time was that of Robert George Pollock White. He had been in Los Angeles at the time of the murder, and was later arrested in San Diego. Here he had attacked an older woman, forcing a cloth down her throat in the manner in which Georgette had been assaulted. But once more, insufficient evidence could be found to charge the man for the heiress's death.

One of the last men to come under scrutiny was one by the name of Kenneth Raymond. Perhaps it was a sign of the desperation the police were suffering from that he was even linked to the crime. Kenneth Raymond was a deserter. He was 23 years old at the time of Georgette's murder and he was actually arrested on suspicion of the kidnap and murder of a six year old girl, Rochelle Gluskoter, earlier in the decade.

In fact he was never convicted of those acts, despite the FBI labelling him a 'one man crime wave'. It seems as though Raymond limited his nefarious activities to robbery and assault. He was questioned about Georgette's murder for just a couple of reasons; he was suspected of crimes against women; he was in Los Angeles at the time and he was very tall; one of the men with whom the heiress had been dancing shortly before her murder was also described as 'tall.'

Perhaps the biggest lift to police in their forlorn pursuit of the perpetrator of this killing came through a confession. The history of crime is littered with false confessions from the strange and ill who wish to be associated with deeds they would never commit. However John Lehman Sumter's story had a ring of truth about it...at least to law enforcement officers desperate for a lead. It was a couple of months after the killing and no further clues had come to light. Perhaps that was not too surprising. It seemed more than likely that the killer was one of the thousands of servicemen who passed through Los Angeles on their way to fight in the war. Almost certainly, they would be gone within a couple of days of the crime, at the very most. Who knows, they may already be dead, killed in action. But Sumter was adamant he was the man responsible. He turned himself into the FBI offices in San Francisco and Deputy Sherriff Hopkinson left to interview him. Sumter claimed that he had met Georgette by chance, on a street car. They had got chatting and Georgette had invited him back to her apartment. Once there, he had persuaded her to make him coffee. A soldier had dropped by, then left after about an hour. Then, for no admitted reason, Sumter had murdered the heiress.

Hopkinson's initial enthusiasm soon waned. While he had heard that Georgette was very friendly and approachable, there was no evidence to suggest that she would invite a stranger back to her apartment late at night. She had a boyfriend; and had just bought a plane ticket to go to visit him. Further, another soldier turning up unannounced in the early hours would imply that she was the kind of girl she clearly was not. Friends were adamant that Georgette was basically shy and retiring, and had clear moral lines she would not cross.

Soon, Sumter withdrew his confession. He claimed that he had made his false admission because he was fed up with living, but was not brave enough to kill himself. Instead, he wanted the state to do it for him. It later turned out that he had previously been committed to a sanitorium.

And so the case wandered on, unsolved. Until, a little over two years later, another crime was committed, and one which resonated to an alarming degree with the murder of Georgette Bauerdorf.

Elizabeth Short was an aspiring actress. She too was young, dark haired and pretty. At the time of her murder, she was also living in Los Angeles. In fact, the links to Georgette go far beyond the physical and geographical. Georgette's day job might have been with the Los Angeles Times, she might have willingly given up her time to be a hostess at the Canteen, but her dream was to become an actress.

Some reports were made at the time that Elizabeth and Georgette were in fact acquaintances, but whether that is true or not is impossible to prove. There were differences between them as well. While Georgette could count on the support of her father's wealth to ensure that she lived a comfortable and affluent life, Elizabeth worked as a waitress while she waited in vain for the big break that would propel her to the halls of super stardom.

If Georgette's murder was violent and horrific, then Elizabeth's was even more so. She was murdered in January of 1947, and was just twenty two years of age. She too was raped and brutalised, but to a much greater extent. Her body was left nude, but mutilated to such a degree that she was cut into two. With a nod to the macabre, she had been drained of blood, then scrubbed clean. Next, the killer had posed her body. She was discovered by a local resident on a vacant lot which was close to Leimert Park in Los Angeles.

Brian Carr was a policeman sent to work on the case and he later described the impact it had made on those close to it. 'It was pretty gruesome,' he said, with carefully controlled understatement. 'I just can't imagine someone doing that to another human being.'

Elizabeth went by the nickname of Black Dahlia; and this innocent enough moniker became morbidly associated with her, to the extent that her own name disappeared behind the mythology that grew up around her assault.

'The case itself took on a life of its own. Early on, I think for two months it was front page news in all the local papers every day,' said Carr.

While the murder was undoubtedly more gruesome than that of Georgette, many commentators saw the likelihood that the two were connected. Certainly, there was no evidence that the perpetrator of the first murder still lived in Los Angeles (after all, it was more than possible he had just been passing through) or even that he had survived the war. But neither case was solved, and maybe the slaughter of Elizabeth was a natural progression in the warped mind of the killer.

Just as Sumter had come forward to claim the 'prize' of being Georgette's killer, so numerous men on the fringes of society sought to take responsibility for this murder. But in none of their confessions did the evidence add up.

Then, fairly recently, there was a development in the Black Dahlia murder at least. Somewhat bizarrely, an author (Steve Hodel) alleged that his father – a doctor - was the killer. But as had been the case throughout, evidence was thin. The accusation was based on no more than gut instinct (we wonder about the son's relationship with his father), an alleged discovery by a dog of human decomposition in a basement, and a possibly overheard conversation in which the doctor's words may be interpreted as those of a killer.

The chances of the murderer of Georgette Bauerdorf still being alive now are remote in the extreme. Even were he just twenty when the crime was carried out, the man would by now be in his mid-nineties. Whether the killer is the same man who ended the life of Elizabeth Short is something that will remain a matter of speculation.

The only certainties with which we are left are that a young woman with a promising future had her life cut short. Perhaps she suspected that she was in danger, as the comments of her friends – and the soldier she picked up on the night in question – implied. Perhaps she knew her killer, and welcomed him into her home. Maybe she even invited him back to her apartment, although that would seem to be out of context considering her normal behaviour. Most likely, it seems, this man had come across the kindly and beautiful Georgette. In all probability this occurred at the Hollywood Canteen. Could he have danced with her that night? Or observed, jealously, some other soldier dancing with her? He had then discovered where she lived – the naïve Georgette was open about her background, and so could well have given away her home details.

Next, he had lain in wait, removing the light from her door so that he could creep up on her. Perhaps he followed her inside, and waited, and her discovery of him was the cause of the dropped tray. Or maybe he disturbed while she was sleeping. So many questions.

When we think back to the black and white days of World War II our views are coloured. They are flavoured by the war films celebrating deeds of bravery and heroism. We see the servicemen as protagonists for good. But they were just men. People caught up in a time not of their choosing.

There were all sorts who went to fight. Not every man saw the Japanese, the Germans or the Italians as their potential victims.

THE REDHEAD MURDERS

JANE CARLISLE

Hey There Little Red Riding Hood...
The Redhead Murders

Hearing about a murder captures our attention. Hearing about a serial killer can put the whole nation on alert. But it is the cases that never get solved, when they get indoctrinated into cult history, that the killer or killers get elevated to an almost more than human status. In these cases there is often barely enough information to tie the murders together, but there are a few chilling continuities that force us to join the dots. It is impossible to know whether it was one person, a group working together, or even copycat murders attempting to emulate the original. This is the case for the Redhead murders.

The Redhead murders may have involved up to eleven women officially, and there are many separate accounts that claim that this number could be almost as high as twenty or thirty women. The main six murders were committed between October 1978 and the 1980s, but it is thought that the murders might have continued through up until 1992 or beyond. The murders occurred throughout the United States, officially including Tennessee, Arkansas, Kentucky, Mississippi, and Pennsylvania, but the movement of the killer has caused many to suggest that his mobile nature implicates him in several other cases with similar circumstances all across the nation. While we don't know much about him, based on potential interactions with the killer by possible surviving victims we do know that he was a middle-aged male. Beyond this, he was incredibly successful at protecting his identity.

The victims, most of whom police were never able to identify, are referred to by the county in which their bodies were dumped. The only connections are that all of them had a reddish hair, some natural and some dyed, and that their bodies were abandoned along major US highways. The fact that they were dumped in this way has caused many to believe that the girls and women were either hitchhikers or prostitutes, and in some cases these backgrounds are confirmed.

However, for some of the girls and women they were not murdered directly on the road, but moved there later. This might suggest that the killer is making a comment about their choices in life, or perhaps left their bodies where he had found them when they were living. What is consistent among them is that the people in the town weren't familiar with the victims, and that no family came forward to identify any of their bodies despite the fact that the cases had national attention. It has therefore been ascertained that the killer was careful in choosing his victims, and that it wasn't purely based on the color of their hair. He wanted to find girls and women who weren't going to have anybody come looking for them, and he succeeded in at least six cases. After the cases in Tennessee, Arkansas, Mississippi, and Pennsylvania, the state police from these areas requested help from the Federal Bureau of Investigation to help to hunt down the murderer, but the main conclusion that came from this interaction was that there were inconsistencies in the cases. Some of the girls and women were found clothing, and others were still dressed. Some had engaged in intercourse before they were murdered, and others hadn't. On this basis, the FBI narrow the amount of victims that they thought were likely to be tied to one killer or set of killers. Several men have been questioned, but all have been subsequently cleared.

For many of the victims, they were found decomposed to the point that their faces could not be recognized. As hair decomposes slower than skin, all that was found of some of the victims was bones, rotten flesh, and red locks. However, police put together all of the information that they could, and did facial reconstructions based on the evidence that was available to them. Several of the women also had missing teeth, but it is not known whether this was the product of poor dental hygiene during life, a struggle with the killer, or a trophy removed from them before they were killed or dumped.

The first of the victims was the one from Wetzel County, her body being found naked on Route 250 just outside of the town of Littleton,

Wetzel County, Virginia. Her body was found on February 13th, 1983 by a pair of senior citizens who initially thought that the body was a mannequin who had fallen out of a truck or been abandoned by the road. However, they then got closer and realized that it was a body. They then called police. Shortly after police arrived, it was determined that she hadn't been left there long before as it was snowing and there hadn't been enough time for a significant amount to accumulate on the woman's body. There was plenty of fresh snow on the ground, and both footprints and tire tracks were visible leading up to and away from the spot. Due to these circumstances, it was determined that she had been murdered elsewhere and moved to the roadside, as her body suggested that she had died two days before. This first victim had not been sexually interfered with, but there were signs that she had been strangled or suffocated. The age range of the victims placed the Wetzel Country victim on the higher end of the scale, as she was estimated to be between the ages of 35 to 45. She was five feet six inches tall (168cm) and weighed 135 pounds (61 kg). There were two distinct scars that were observed on her body after the autopsy, one of these being a scar on her abdomen from a Cesarean section and the other being on one of her index fingers. She was very well groomed and upset, causing police to think that she was not a hitchhiker or in the habit of moving around. The victim may have been seen in Wheeling, West Virginia as an employee or customer at a bar, but this lead was not certain enough to be confirmed. A man was seen near the place where the body was found, and suspicions arose that he was responsible for the murder of the woman and disposal of her body. He was a white male who was approximately five feet ten inches tall (178 cm) and weighed between 185 and 300 pounds (84-91kg). This sighting has shaped the claims against several suspects over the years after they have been involved in the kidnapping and rape of redheaded women.

The second victim, Lisa Nichols, was 28 years old and sometimes went by the name of Jarvis. She was found on the 16th September 1984 on the Interstate 40 close to West Memphis, Arkansas. She lived in West Virginia, but authorities were not able to get into contact with her family for nearly a year. During this period of time, she could not be identified and it is assumed that she was estranged from her family. Nichols was left only wearing a sweater, and had strawberry-blonde hair. She was identified in June of 1985 by a couple from Florida who had have her stay with them for a period of time when she was on the move. She was found close to a truck stop, and it is assumed that she was standing on the road attempting to hitchhike close to this truck stop when she was picked up by her killer.

On 1st January 1985, the third victim considered to be tied to the case was found close to Jellico, Tennessee in Campbell County on Interstate 75. It was determined that she had been killed three days prior to when she was found, but it was determined that she was in an advanced state of decomposition. As it was with the others, she was white and had red hair. This victim was approximately between the ages of 17 and 25, but it has been estimated by some sources that she might have been almost 30 years old at the time that she died. She was found fully clothed with a tan pullover, a shirt, and jeans. Her eye color could not be determined due to decomposition, and she was determined to be between 2 ½ and 5 months pregnant. She was too decomposed for authorities to estimate her weight, but it is thought that at the time of death she would have been five feet four inches (163cm) and 110 to 115 pounds (50 – 52kg).

The body of the second Campbell County victim was discovered on the 3rd April 1985, but her hair color was not known. However, due to the time period and other circumstances related to her murder and the disposal of her body, many sources consider this case to be related to the other Redhead murders. It was estimated that she had died between 1981 and 1984, one to four years before her body was found. She was estimated to be ages between 9 and 15 years old, making her the youngest potential case to be connected with these murders. The body was found by a passerby around 200 yards away from Big Wheel Gap Road, which is four miles southwest of Jellico in Campbell County, the same town that the first Campbell County victim was found near. Many have taken this information as a sign that this is where the killer either began his murders, or a place that he called home for a time in his life. The cause of her death is unknown as her remains were only partial, but it was still determined that she was the victim of a homicide. The sit contained 32 bones, including her skull which allows for facial reconstruction. She was wearing a necklace and a bracelet made from plastic clothing buttons, and there were a pair of size five boots and a few scraps of clothing. It was not possible to determine her weight, eye color, or hair color due to the length of time that had passed since her murder.

Just before the discovery of the second Campbell County victim was a body found on the 31st March 1985 in Pleasant View, Cheatham County, Tennessee. Her body was nothing but a skeleton, but her hair remained. It is thought that she had died three to five months beforehand, due to a cause that could not be determined from her remains. However, her body was found on the side of the highway Interstate 24 wearing a shirt, sweater, pants, and underwear. She was between five feet and five feet two inches (around 157 cm tall) and her weight could not be determined from her remains. She is thought to have been between the ages of 31 and 40 at the time of her death.

Another body was found on 1st April 1985 in Gray, Knox County, Kentucky on Route 25. She had been suffocated and stuffed into a white Admiral refrigerator, and a decal of the words Super Woman was on the front of the appliance. She was naked aside from two necklaces with pendants that she was wearing, one of them a heart and the other a gold-colored eagle. She was also wearing two pairs of socks, one of them white and the other pair white with green and yellow stripes. Some sources report that the victim was trying to get a lift to North Carolina over CB radio. The discovery threw the usually sleepy town of Gray into confusion, and was a point of high discussion. Five hundred people attended the woman's funeral, and it was televised in an attempt to ask people to come forward with any information about the woman or her attacker. The woman had several distinctive moles, a yellowed upper incisor, and a scar from a Caesarian just as had been the case with the first victim in Wetzel County. The fact that so many of these girls and women were pregnant early on in their life or had already had a baby has not been used to tie them together, but may have been considered when placing their line of work as prostitution. The Knox County victim was between 24 to 35 years old and four feet nine inches to four feet eleven inches tall, and 100 pounds (45 kg). There was a pair of boots found near the refrigerator, and it is possible that these belonged to the victim. Several missing persons cases were cross-referenced in an attempt to identify the woman, but all of the were dismissed. When the case was re-publicized in January of 2013, some tips came forward with information but it is unknown whether these tips turned into any solid leads.

On 14th April, the body of a girl between 14 and 20 years of age was found in Greenville, Greene County, Tennessee. She had died between three and six weeks before her body was discovered and she was in an advanced state of decomposition. Despite the condition of her body, it was still possible to get her fingerprints, DNA, and dental information. It was determined from her remains that she had died of blunt-force trauma, and potentially a stab wound. She was also 6 to 8 weeks pregnant before she died, but had recently miscarried. She had a slight overbite and fillings, which suggested that she had had dental care in her life. She was five feet four inches tell (168 cm) and between 130 to 140 pounds (59 – 64kg). Her fingernails were painted pink and she had light brown to blonde hair with red highlights. Authorities were hopeful that they would be able to identify her using fingerprints, but their attempt was unsuccessful. She has still not been identified up to present, and six women thought to be her were rules out as possible identities.

Aside from these six victims, there were also several others that were considered as potentially connected to the case. One of these was the Rising Fawn Jane Doe who was found in 1988 in Georgia. She was between 16 and 25 years old and was found on the roadside near Interstate 59. The victim was between five feet six inches and five feet eight inches (approximately 168 cm), and was between 120 – 125 pounds (54 – 56 kg). She had no distinctive tattoos or scars, but strawberry/brownish red hair. She was found wearing an extra large, Navy blue, thermaknit, long-sleeved pullover, a navy blue bra, Calvin Klein jeans, and black, size 9, lace-up, ankle-high shoes. She was wearing a yellow gold chain around her neck and a white gold pinkie ring on her left finger with a heart on the top of it. She was sexually abused by her murderer, and investigators felt that she was someone who would have been travelling through as she found was so close to the Georgia/Alabama state line.

Another potential victim of the Redhead murders was the Desoto County Jane Doe who was found on January 24th 1985 in Olive Branch, Desoto County, Mississippi. She had died only hours before she was found, meaning that her face was recognizable. She was 20 to 35 years old and killed by strangulation or exposure. She had three piercings in each ear, deeply bitten finger nails, was a heavy smoker, had her tubes tied, and had a small frame with a freckled complexion. She had two tattoos, T. H. C on her right ankle, and R. C. J, R. E. J, or R. E. T. on her left ankle. She also had a diagonal surgical scar 12 cm long on the back of her left forearm, a scar on the pop joint of her left hand, scars on her second and third fingers, and a scar at the base of her thumb. Her teeth were in poor conditions with one missing on the bottom row at the front. She was found with a light peach-colored, short-sleeved pullover with embroidery on the front, and Gloria Vanderbilt jeans. She had no shoes, no coat, and no undergarments. The body was spotted at 7:30 AM by a truck driver travelling southbound on Interstate 78, east of the Coldwater River Bridge.

The last potential victim with a significant amount of information on her was the Pulaski County Jane Doe found in Wrightsville, Arkansas on April 20th 1985. She had decomposed to the point that she was not recognizable, and only a partial skeleton was found. The cause of her death was unknown. The woman was between the ages of 30 and 40 years old, and she was found face-down in a river with her clothes 70 feet southwest near the river bank.

Other possible victims are the Pemiscot County Doe who was found in Arkansas in 1978, the Hawayr County Jane Doe identified as Priscilla Ann Blevins, the Roane County Jane Doe sound in 1987, the Benton County Jane Doe found in 1990, the Hebron Jane Doe found in Ohio in 1990, and the Simpson County Jane Doe found in Tennessee in 2001. There were also several more potential cases in Texas, but they were considered to have too many inconsistencies with the other cases to be linked to the same killer or set of killers. There are also many accounts online of people who feel that they have interacted with the killer. One of these instances is from a woman who had a man approach her and her mother when they were travelling in Texas when she was eight, making the comment that she should never leave her unattended because there are men that hurt little girls with hair like hers. Another example of that of a remark from a man at the Frontier House Gift Shop and Restaurant in Jellico, Tennessee, at the time of several of the murders in the town where two of the victims were found. The waitress, who dyed her hair auburn, had a man comment on her hair and then say that he was "coming back".

There have been three main suspects for the Redhead murders over the years, but all three men were cleared after questioning. The first of these was a 37 year old truck driver Jerry Leon Johns who had attacked and attempted to strangle a woman with reddish hair, Linda Schacke.

He had met her at a nude dancing club. He left her lying in a storm drain near a highway under the assumption that she was dead, but he was later dismissed as having any connection with the other murders. Ms. Schacke had her torn shirt tied around her neck and was thrown into a culvert alongside Interstate 40, and was able to identify Johns as her attacker. John felt that police were attempting to "brand" him as the Redhead murderer, and maintains that he was not involved in any of the slayings. After this, a 32 year old truck driver in Pennsylvania, Thomas Lee Elkins, was questioned after he kidnapped and raped a 20 year old woman from Boston before she managed to escape from him and went to police. She ran away while he was sleeping and called for help from a farmhouse. She had been bound by hand and foot and kept prisoner, but she had managed to get loose of her bindings. However, this suspect was cleared after being questioned by Tennessee police. While Elkins was not considered to be responsible for the Redhead murders, he was arrested for his treatment of the woman that he had kidnapped and raped, and was put in the Dyer County jail without bond. Finally, a 27 year old Tracy Lee Housel who was arrested 14th April 1985 in Daytona Beach was charged with raping and murdering a Lawrenceville woman the week before and dumping her body by an interstate. He told Georgia police that he had also killed two women near Interstate 75 north of Knoxville, but there were reportedly no connections between Housel and the Redhead victim in Knoxville. There were also two more potential suspects, Henry Lee Lucas and Ottis Toole, but they were ruled out when it was confirmed that they were in jail at the time of many of the killings. Lucas faced the death penalty in Texas and Toole was sentences to death in Florida.

Phillip W. Johnson, a psychologist at the Kentucky Correctional Psychiatric Center at the Luther Luckett Correctional Complex at La Grange, commented on two potential reasons for why the serial killer might be targeting young, white women with red hair. "I would wonder if the red hair didn't symbolize one of two extremes: what the person wanted and couldn't have or what the person wanted to rid himself of," he said, making reference to a partner that he might have had in the past, or a woman that he might have been lusting over. "Is the person killing out of anger or is the person involved in a symbolic joining between the victim and her killer? Perhaps it's the redheaded girlfriend who rejected the individual or the redheaded mother." Considering that the killer also seems to have targeting many women who were pregnant or with children, there might be a connection to the little girl that was the second Campbell County victim. Could this have been a relation to the man, or potentially even his child? Could there have been an individual that sparked off this seemingly specific targeting and disposing of women with similar pasts? After each of the murders, many redheaded women or families with redheaded girls contacted their local police, terrified that they or their family members would be targeted next.

The reason that this killer or set of killers may have had such success with not getting caught is due to the victims that they targeted. Agent David Davenport of the Tennessee Bureau of Investigations commented that "The problem is, these women are mostly hitchhikers or prostitutes with no strong family ties. Nobody is looking for them. Most times nobody cares. What we're facing is that most of the victims are unidentified. And if they're unidentified, you can't go back and see who they were with last." As nobody has ever been caught for the killings, there are often claims by online amateur sleuths and news stations that more recent deaths may also be a part of the Redhead murders. If there are any young women with red hair who have died under suspicious circumstances, their deaths are often attributed to this murderer or murderers even if they have not been dumped by a major highway road. It has now been enough time that it is highly likely that this mystery will never be solved, as the murders occurred so long ago and to people who did not have families demanding justice for the deaths. If the killer was in his prime in the seventies and eighties, it is possible that he may no longer even be alive. And while there will be many discussions about the three keys suspects and their potential involvement in the case, it is now unlikely that anybody will be coming forward with any new information that might lead to the arrest of anybody in connection to these murders. Unfortunately, the way that all of these women are likely to be remembered is for their connection with this case and the circumstances in which they died. However, it is possible that these events and others like them have boosted national awareness about the dangers of hitchhiking as it has become a much less frequent practice as the decades have gone by. Whether these young girls and women were hitchhikers or prostitutes, the circumstances of their deaths were tragic. If nobody is ever found to be responsible for their deaths, it is important to learn from these experiences as a nation and educate young women about the potential dangers that they might face in their lives, particularly those who might not be in a situation where they have a community of people to look out for them.

GENENE JONES : NURSE KILLER

TAMI BARRETT

Genene Anne Jones was born on July 13th, 1950 in Texas but was given up for adoption. Her adopted parents had three other children. Two were older and one was younger than Genene.

EARLY LIFE

Her adopted parents were Richard and Gladys Jones. Richard, better known as "Dick", a night club and was a gambler. He was a big spender and generous when he was flush. His club was called the Kit Kat Swim Club, the place had a dance floor with a patio and pool outside. His wife Gladys was the disc jockey at the club and the couple lived an extravagant lifestyle. They had a mansion that looked down on San Antonio, would travel often and they would both have pilot licenses .

At the age of ten, however, Genene's father was arrested for stealing the safe of a customer who had been at Jones' club at the time of the robbery. These charges were later dropped.

It could have been due to intimidation on Dick's part. The man was six feet tall, weighed a solid 240 pounds and was bold. He had an aggressive demeanor when needed and his adopted daughter developed the same traits.

His business soon failed, however. The shady Kit Kat Club soon turned into a family themed restaurant which put Dick further into debt. He then sold off the restaurant and earned a living putting up billboards around San Antonio. Genene would later describe helping her father put up the billboards as one of the happier times of her life.

Still, Genene felt as if she suffered from neglect in the adopted home. The parents had paired off the four kids on the basis of age. Genene had an older brother Wiley and an older sister named Lisa. She had a younger brother named Travis who had a learning disability that she doted on and cared for. Nonetheless, she felt jealous of all the attention that Lisa would receive. Genene referred to herself as the "black sheep" of the family and took out her frustrations on her classmates at school. She worked in the library at John Marshall and was described as "kind of bossy" by the high school librarian as she would berate other student volunteers who weren't doing their jobs up to her standards. Short and chubby, Genene felt unattractive and began to become known for lying and manipulating people.

"Lying was like talking for her," one of her classmates recalled as Genene would often tell people that she was related to Micky Dolenz, the band member of the Monkees, and that she would routinely have phone conversations with him all the time.

Tragedy would strike in her teens, however, when her younger brother Travis died in a freak accident.

He had put together a pipe bomb which exploded in his face, sending metal shards into his head. Genene took the loss hard, arriving at the funeral with a large flower wreath, crying hysterically, then feinting.

"You wonder when Genene's mind got twisted," forensic psychologist Dina Foster said. "It had to have been early on in her development when somehow, someway she got a surge of power when she was care taking for someone particularly a child. This was probably her brother, Travis. Being a caregiver for him made her feel important. She realized that she could be respected and have people look up to her until it became twisted."

A year later, her father died of cancer at the age of 56 which further devastated Genene. She had yet to graduate high school and wanted to get married. Her adopted mother refused as she Genene's choice of mate, a dropout named James "Jimmy" Harvey Delany Jr as nothing but trouble.

The two would marry, however, and live in a guesthouse near the mansion. Jimmy, however, was only interested in cars and drinking. The two would squabble often until Jimmy decided to join the Navy. With her husband away a basic training, Genene would not remain faithful, going after both single and married men. She had an affair with the newlywed husband of a former high school classmate. Then she began to tell people she had been sexually abused as a child. After four years of marriage, Genene divorced Jimmy as she stated that he had been physically abusive toward her.

Genene would threaten divorce but the two would reconcile.

"She experienced abandonment twice," Foster said. "The first go around was when her mother gave her up for adoption. The second go around was when her brothers and father died back to back. She had lost two loved ones to illnesses and one to a tragic accident. She felt helpless and out of control. But unlike most people, Genene went the criminal route in order to assuage the pain. She had to do things to get the power and control back."

CAREER LIFE & DIVORCE

Genene entered Mim's Beauty School and became a beautician, finding work at the Methodist Hospital beauty parlor. She had her first child, Richard, in 1972 while she and Jimmy were stationed in Georgia. They would move back to San Antonio but by that time the marriage was failing. She filed for divorce in Bexar County, eight months after Richard was born and stated that her husband was "a man of violent and ungovernable temper and passion" while also accusing him of "unconscionable brutality and physical cruelty." She won a court order that forbade her husband from going near both her or baby Richard. Two months later, however, the couple had gotten back together and the judge threw out the divorce suit.

"Clearly they had an on and off again relationship," Foster said. "Jimmy was hapless, wanting to do nothing more than race cars and party. So in some aspects Genene had found her soul mate, a man who needed taking care of."

But on June 3rd, 1974, Genene filed for divorce again and the couple would battle in the court system for three more years. She would file suit against Delany for failure to pay child support and in August of 1976 she won a contempt citation against him. In March of 1977, both consented to drop the legal battle and in July 17 of 1977 Genene's second child, Heather, was born. She later admitted that Heather had been conceived out of wedlock when she and Delany had another brief coming to terms.

Genene would then move back in with her adopted mother who helped with the babies as she began her training at San Antonio Independent School District's School of Vocational Nursing. Genene was a mediocre high school student but she excelled in the program, earning high grades. She aced the licensing exam and got a job at Methodist Hospital.

Genene only lasted eight months, however, getting fired when she made decisions about patient care in which she had no authority as well as being rude to patients. Genene would later claim that she was fired for standing up to a doctor who was being rude to a patient.

"She was a compulsive liar when she was a kid," Foster said. "And the lying continued into her adult life as it turned into full blown denial. She was never at fault for anything. It was always someone else, doctors, nurses, her mother, her husband. She never lived in the land of responsibility."

REIGN OF TERROR BEGINS

Genene then found work at Bexar County Hospital (now known as the University Hospital of San Antonio) where she was assigned to the Pediatric ICU.

It is here where the trouble officially began.

Her first patient had a fatal stomach disease called necrotizing enterocolitis and the boy died after surgery. Genene did not handle it well, crying hysterically. "She just went berserk," Cherylyn Pendergraft said, the RN that was orienting Genene during this time. Genene went so far as to move a stool toward the baby's cubicle and just sat there staring at the body.

Pendergraft felt the gesture odd considering that Genene had barely cared for the child.

Nonetheless, Genene saw herself as an equal to the RN's on duty and worked extra hard to acquire more knowledge than an ordinary LVN.

She worked the graveyard shift upon hire then transferred to the swing shift where she worked f3 p.m to 11 p.m while frequently volunteering for overtime and extra shifts.

Genene soon took on a reputation as the "nurse who cried wolf" to the many resident doctors who were training at the hospital. She would issue warnings about a child's worsening condition to the intern. If the intern did nothing she would then go to the resident doctor. If that physician did nothing then she would go higher up the chain of command and wouldn't stop until her recommendations were addressed.

Despite her eagerness to be perceived as on the same level as a registered nurse, Genene would skip continuation classes on the proper use of pharmaceuticals. In her first year, she was written up on eight separate occasions for giving the wrong dosage.

Genene wouldn't let any reprimands stop her, however, as she soon became the ward bully in the cramped quarters of the pediatric ICU. She would intimidate other nurses with her coarse demeanor, making more than a few transfer out of the unit to get away from her.

Her bullying tactics enabled her to make the unit her own, as she was the foul-mouthed Queen of the ward, bragging about her sexual escapades and making inappropriate remarks.

"Here we see the beginnings of tacit approval," Foster said. "No one at the hospital wants to put themselves on the line to stand up against her. It is an environment where everyone is trying to cover their own ass. No one wants to play snitch even when this woman is saying and doing all of these inappropriate things."

Even more disturbing is that Genene would also predict which baby would die.

During "report", a time in which the nurses would describe the conditions of their patients during the shift change handover to the next nurse, Genene would play the role of the Grim Reaper.

"This patient is really bad," she'd say forewarning the nurse, or even predicting death." This patient isn't going to make it."

By 1981, Genene would always demand to be assigned to the sickest patients. She seemed to enjoy the adrenaline rush of the code blues and would grieve when the child expired. Genene would hold the dead bodies and sing to it, making sure she would be the one to take the corpse to the morgue.

"She had a twisted hero complex," Foster said. "She thought of herself as equal to any RN. Most LVNs defer to the registered nurses out of education and experience. But it was quite the opposite with Genene. When the shit hit the fan she would be the first to come to the rescue. The problem was that she created these situations where she could be seen as the hero. Remember she didn't give them enough medication to kill them outright. She gave the babies just enough of a dose so that they would go into cardiac arrest. She wanted to be seen as the savior to the parents of the children she was killing. She wanted to be seen as the hero of the ward. This need was so deep-seated that she was willing to kill to get that need met. That need to be seen as a hero. That need to be seen as the most compassionate of all."

TOO MANY PATIENTS DYING

Co-workers became concerned that a surprising number of patients under the care of Jones were dying.

"The other nurses became concerned," said Vincent J.M. Dimaio, the chief medical examiner at the time. "That there were increased numbers of cardiopulmonary arrests on the ward. All her victims were children. The most innocent of the population. This would not have happened if the cases had been reported to the medical examiner's office."

Unlike most hospitals, Bexar County didn't lock their medications in a cabinet. When it become apparent that children were dying in the unit from non-fatal illnesses, the hospital dragged its feet in an investigation. There was a two-week period where seven children died in the unit. These deaths occurred only when Genene Jones was on duty and the patients were under her care.

"Astonishing," Foster said. "The tacit approval now extended to the cover up of children being murdered. The hospital administrators put their own public relations and jobs above the lives of children. It is a travesty of justice that no one at the hospital was ever punished for this."

Genene had an ally in the department in the form of Dr. James Robotham, however. Known as "JR", a reference to the ruthless businessman from the TV show Dallas, Robotham was an aggressive doctor throughout his tenure in the ICU. He had no problem dressing down nurses or student doctors who were not up to snuff or did not bend to his will. He had no hiring authority in the hospital but took on a vital role throughout the ICU by placing the patient's care onto his shoulders.

Genene saw a kindred spirit in Robotham and the doctor took a liking to her. There was one occasion in which he needed assistance and chose Genene over another nurse.

"She had been validated," Foster said. "She also wanted to be acknowledged for her nursing talents and finally there was someone who came along and anointed her as someone who was worthy."

"Robotham's Pet" as some of the nurses would later call her, would nonetheless display a macabre interest when a child came in with a fatal illness. Genene would make it clear that she wanted to be on hand when death inevitably came.

Genene would enjoy calling the parents to inform them of their child's death, sharing in their grief over the phone.

"She was Jekyll and Hyde," Foster said. "With the nurses and staff she would be coarse, demanding and condescending. But with the parents of the children she turned into the ultimate caregiver. Soft-spoken, compassionate, and joining them in their pain. She would have the parents believing that she was the most caring person on the face of the earth."

Never mind the fact that she would orchestrate the medical emergency of the child.

"That was her way of getting attention," Dimaio said. "She was a 'big person'. She was a 'big person' when she resuscitated children. When she brought them back from death's door. And the rest of her life, she wasn't anything."

THE KILLINGS MOUNT

A six month old baby named Jose Antonio Flores came into the unit with non-fatal symptoms: fever, vomiting and diarrhea. Unfortunately, he came under the care of Genene.

The baby soon suffered a seizure went into cardiac arrest and died.

Genene grabbed the dead baby and ran out of the department with the staff having to track down the crying LVN. The infant was later blood-tested and the results revealed that there had been an overdose of heparin, an anti-coagulant.

No one had ordered that the drug be administered and now the staff became suspicious.

When questioned about the baby's death, Genene resorted to manipulation and blackmail. She told the staff that she took records on every child that had died there and she knew which doctor had killed them.

Finally, one of the doctors informed the hospital administration what he suspected of Genene Jones. He had found a book in her possession about how to inject heparin through the skin without leaving a mark.

The hospital administrators, however, did not want the bad public relations fall out that would result from being a hospital that had a reputation for infant deaths.

"Say that they expected one (death) a week," Dimaio said. "All of a sudden they were getting three or four or five a week. I don't think there was any doubt that they had a good idea of what she (Genene) was doing."

"The amazing thing here is that even after the incident with the Flores' baby, Genene was allowed to continue working on the ward," Foster said.

Another child came into Genene's unit, this time to recover from open heart surgery. The child made progress but during Genene's shift he died.

"They notice that all of them (the deaths) were on the same shift," Dimaio said. "And all of them involved patients being taken care of by Genene Jones."

More doctors complained and a committee was set up to investigate. Head nurse Pat Belko and James Robotham were in charge on the hospital end but an outside team of investigators came in to look at the problem.

This third party team declined to put the blame on Genene as their findings were inconclusive.

COVERING THEIR ASS

Confident of they were in the clear, the hospital reports no abnormal deaths to the county medical examiner. Still, the hospital knew that Genene Jones was responsible for the deaths.

"She was left on the ward even though they knew what was going on," Dimaio said. "Someone said why don't we just fire her? Then they said well she'll just sue us and they'll be a big scandal. There were more interested in saving their reputation and not being sued then in the life and health of these children."

In order to avoid a public relations debacle, the administration decided to replace the LVNs in the unit with registered nurses. They said they were raising the "training bar" for ICU nurses and that LVNs would no longer be needed.

"So when they adopted that policy they let her go from that unit," Dimaio said. "Let go by the way, with an excellent letter of recommendation. Even though they knew what was going on."

Genene had been suspected in the deaths of over 47 other children, the NYT noted that the administration of Bexar County Medical Center and the University of Texas Medical school had shredded over 9,000 pounds of pharmaceutical records, records that were created during the time when Jones worked there.

By doing this, these administrators effectively destroyed any evidence that would be helpful in convicting Genene Jones of more crimes. The hospital stated that the shredding of documents was "routine" and a "coincidence", but the district attorney was able to intervene when, acting on a tip from an informant, he stopped the hospital from destroying an additional 50,000 pounds of pharmaceutical and medical records. The dean of medicine at Bexar was then cited for contempt of court when it was discovered that she withheld hospital reports from the grand jury.

"This is certainly an indictment of the hospital," Foster said. "If over 47 children were murdered, than there would have to be justice. The irony here is that the hospital administrators are not that far off from Genene Jones' mindset. They lie, deny and keep things in secret. All for the sake of control. All for the sake of being perceived that they are something they are not. Genene wanted to be seen as a hero but was really a killer. The hospital wants good pr at all costs, even childcare's lives. They are scum."

THE MURDERS CONTINUE

After her release from the county hospital and with a letter of recommendation in hand, Jones found work at a pediatric physician's clinic in Kerrville, Texas.

"She ended up here in Kerrville after she left San Antonio because of all these unexplained deaths," district attorney Ron Sutton said. "Genene Jones absolutely despises me because I brought down her little self-constructed impact."

The clinic was a start-up to be run by Dr. Kathleen Holland. She only had budget for an LVN and immediately thought of Genene Jones. She had remembered Genene and had been impressed by her take-charge personality and competence.

Holland contacted the human resource office at the hospital and inquired about the availability of Genene. Holland knew about the strange rumors about Genene but was willing to overlook them as she needed someone who could bring passion to their start up.

Holland didn't know how true those weird rumors were..

"She would create these medical emergencies," District Attorney Ron Sutton said. "That only she would know to handle. Then she would look like this supreme nurse when she would take care of the emergencies that she created."

Holland's revelation began with Petti McClellan brought in her young daughter Chelsea. McClellan said that Chelsea had a "bad cold" and went into the exam room with Dr. Holland. Genene then took the young baby out of Chelsea's arms, stating that she was going to "play" with the baby so that she and the doctor could talk.

"She had an irresistible compulsion," Foster said. "Doesn't matter where she is at, a hospital, a clinic, she has that compulsion. She'll see the opportunity to be a create the scenario for herself and she takes it."

"The protocol for the doctor's office would be the nurse, Genene Jones, would take the baby into a separate room just she and the baby, to perform whatever cursory examination; weight, blood pressure, whatever," Sutton said. "But during the time Genene would have these children by themselves all of a sudden they would become like a rag doll. And then she would scream out 'the baby's not breathing.'"

Moments later, Genene would cry out for help, saying that the baby couldn't breathe.

Doctor Holland immediately jumped into action, seeing that the baby had gone into a seizure. The child would be transported to a hospital and her life was spared.

The McClellan's expressed their gratitude toward Holland and Genene. They thought the world of the duo, believing that they saved the life of their child.

Little did they know that Genene had injected the child with succinylcholine.

Genene had used various methods to kill children under her care. She used injections of digoxin, heparin and later succinylcholine to cause a "code blue" in her patients. She would revive them afterward and receive praise. The succinylcholine she used is a paralytic that causes a temporary paralysis of skeleton muscles which can affect a patient's breathing. When she injected small children with this drug, the victim would suffer from cardiac arrest.

Petti would later return to the clinic months later with Chelsea. She had actually called the clinic to make an appointment for her son Cameron but Holland insisted that she bring Chelsea in so that she could "check on her."

"My daughter wasn't sick," Petti would later say.

Holland later disputes the claim that she asked Petti to bring Chelsea in instead of Cameron.

Unfortunately, Petti would bring Chelsea in and witness Genene administer two shots. The second shot would cause Chelsea to go into a seizure and later die.

"Once she began doing it," Foster said. "She couldn't stop. She became fueled by the adrenaline. The rush she got by sticking the syringe into the baby. The rush she got in waiting for the child to go into cardiac arrest. The the rush she got by watching the child die and comforting it in its death. She even got off on informing the parents of the baby's death. That is how twisted her mind was."

"Her original intent may not have been to kill," Foster said. "She was all about being seen as the hero, the Superwoman who came into save the day. Why she would target the same child coming in for another routine check-up really shows that she was getting careless about her victims. She had gotten away with it for so long that she didn't care. Plus, the compulsion would override whatever logic and forward thinking she had."

Chelsea's death was initially seen as sudden infant death syndrome.

"That's when we talked to the anesthesiologist," Sutton said. "He said that this child looks like it was coming out from the effects of succinylcholine, and we launched our investigation at that point."

"Soon as she got that first shot," Petti McClellan said, "Chelsey immediately starting reacting to it. And I asked her right off the bat, 'what did you do? What did you do? Something's wrong with her.'."

Genene visited Chelsey's grave and seemed genuinely remorseful.

"She was a psychopath with conflicted emotions," Foster said. "On one hand she had this need to kill and be in control of what others thought of her, specifically as a hero. And the other hand, she may have felt remorse when her 'heroic' efforts didn't produce the results she wanted."

Chelsey's mother, Petti, however, was shocked to see Genene at her daughter's grave.

Holland would later find puncture marks in a bottle of succinylcholine in a storage cabinet that only she and Genene had access to. "There were two holes in the lid of this bottle," Sutton said. "One where she had withdrawn and then she attempted to replace it with saline solution."

With the investigators closing in, Genene began to panic. She arrived at the clinic after lunch and complained to Holland that she was feeling ill...She had overdosed on her anti-depressants and began looking lethargic.

Holland immediately called the paramedics and Genene's stomach was pumped. Later upon her release, Texas Ranger Joe Davis interrogated her about the holes in the bottle of succinylcholine. Genene denied involvement, stating that she would be willing take a polygraph test.

The next day, Holland was shocked to see Genene report for work as if nothing had happened. She then informed Genene that her services would no longer be needed. Genene grew enraged and challenged Holland to take a polygraph. She then stormed out of the office.

Genene would later call back to the office and informed Holland's secretary that she had left a letter for the physician in her drawer.

The letter was a one page suicide note that she had written before she had taken the overdose of anti-depressants.

"There isn't anyway to explain to you why things are going to change. Sometimes, as wrong as it may seem, you have to except what life dishes out.

When your older, and I know your tired of hearing that, but you will be able to understand why, why I have to go away. It doesn't mean I don't love you. Please believe that. No amount of money or worldly goods could every buy my love. It is so deep & strong, it will last for all eternity.

Please explain if you can to Heather & Michael how much I love them. It's such a strong love, I can't put it on paper. I know I'm asking a lot, but I really feel your the only one who could do it.

I'm not guilty of murder, & I hope you believe that. But Daddy's way is right. It takes all the pressure off you and the seven people whose life I have altered.

No one can hurt me with my Daddy. He'll straighten this whole thing out & then we'll go home & everything will be alright. No more problems for you, no more nightmares for me.

Please make sure Michael and Heather are not separated. I know how my mother feels about Heather, but I also know how she feels about Michael. If Debbie or you can't take them together, please be sure whoever does are good people. People with lots of love.

Please don't be angry. I'm going with Daddy because I miss him and I want to be with him. He'll take care of both of us.

You'll be fine. Please believe that.

I love you,

Genene

Genene had attempted to frame Holland for the murders but all evidence pointed to her. All said and done, Genene had poisoned at least six children at the clinic. Three of the parents continued to utilize Holland as their pediatrician while three other families sued both Holland and Genene Jones as they believed that Holland knew or should have known about Genene's murderous ways.

The criminal investigation began and Chelsea's body was exhumed, revealing traces of the succinylcholine.

Her exact numbers of victims remain unknown as hospital officials first "misplaced" then destroyed records of her activities to prevent lawsuits after Genene's first conviction.

Genene would go on trial on January 15th, 1984 for the murder of Chelsea and injury to the other children. On February, 15, 1984, Genene was convicted of murder after a three hour deliberation. She was given the maximum sentence of ninety-nine years. In October, she went on trail for injuring Rolando Jones with an injection of heparin. She was sentenced a total of 159 years with the possibility of parole that came up after serving ten years.

In 1985, Gene was sentenced to 99 years in prison for killing fifteen month old Chelsea McClellan.

Later that year, she was sentenced to a term of sixty years in prison for the attempted murder of Rolando Jones with heparin.

"I've had several cases that stand out in my mind," Sutton said. "But this one is particularly heinous because of death to small children.

SERIAL KILLER TO BE RELEASED

Genene Jones is now set to go free because of a legal loophole in the form of She is now scheduled for mandatory release in February 2018 due to a Texas law that prevents prison overcrowding. Genene has been a prisoner who has exhibited "good behavior", becoming eligible for the release.

"Please, please, please, do not let this person walk," Petti McClellan said.

"Genene Jones is probably one of the worst types of serial killers because keep in mind who her victims were," said Andy Kahan, a victim advocate. "Defenseless, voiceless, babies. One of the nation's most diabolical serial killers in our country's history is set to be legally released,"

"I was so angry that it went on for so long," Cherlyn Pendergraft said. "That so many children had to die."

Jones now claims to be sickly and is housed in medical jail unit.

"Am I prepared that she walks?" McClellan asked. "No. Because she's gonna hurt another child. I don't want to hear that she's sick. Or that she's old, she's two years older than I am."

"There is absolutely no reason for Genene Jones to be walking the streets," Foster said. "She has a compulsion that has to be satiated. She needs to be locked up for the rest of her life."

The current District Attorney is looking to re-open old cases against Jones in order to keep her in prison.

She Killed Dad

Jessi Dillard

Born on May 28, 1972, Stacey Ann Lannert grew up in what appeared to be a picture-perfect family. She and her sister, Christy, were raised by two loving parents. Tom, their father, worked as a financial consultant, and their mother Deb took on the role of a stay-at-home mom. However, as the two girls got older, their 'ideal' family started to crumble right before their eyes.

"In 1990, life as I knew it ended, for better and for worse," Lannert wrote in her memoir, *Redemption: A Story of Sisterhood, Survival, and Finding Freedom Behind Bars*. "I had committed murder."

Daddy's little girl

In the early 70s, the Lannert family lived in Cedar Rapids, Iowa. Deb was a devoted mother, Lannert recalled in her memoir. As a stay-at-home mom, she kept up with the regular domestic chores, but also spent a lot of time teaching her young daughter. Lannert learned her ABCs by the age of two, and at three, could write her telephone number and her name. Before she turned four years old, she knew how to read.

"We had all of her attention in the early years," Lannert wrote. "I wish we could have frozen time and just stayed in that place forever."

However, Lannert recalls being particularly close to her father – even describing herself as "daddy's little girl." Her father was "like Superman" to her, because he was always prepared to handle any problem she encountered. She remembers him as handsome, with a prominent nose and a strong chin, and a warm, comforting laugh.

"He had beautiful blue eyes that could melt or destroy me – it was his choice," she said. "We stayed up late together even when I was really little. He held me all the time when he finished work or studying."

After dinner, they would share a snack of buttered popcorn from her dad's special yellow Tupperware bowl. He referred to his eldest daughter as "Tiger," and always encouraged her to stand up for herself whenever the kids at school teased her.

"I always felt like everything was right in the world when he was there," she said. "He lavished me with attention, and I could see no wrong in my father. He was just *it* for me."

The family's life was so idyllic, so secure and happy that Lannert said she didn't pay much notice to the "tiny cracks" that were beginning to form in the family's foundation. A car accident that should have killed Tom left him with nothing more than a few scratches, thanks to his blood alcohol level.

"His body was so loose from the alcohol that he slithered right out of the car," Lannert recalled. "He didn't even remember what had happened."

It's not a big deal, she remembers her father telling her. "Everything is going to be fine."

But things weren't fine. The more Tom would drink, the more Deb would nag – and Lannert said the bond she and her father shared became even stronger as his marriage began to fall apart. And when Deb gave away Lannert's beloved dog, Max, she said she started to think her mother was just mean.

"Twenty years later, I found out the truth," she said. "She gave Max away because my dad would come home drunk, trip over my excited dog, and then kick Max. Mom felt awful when she heard the dog yelping in the hallway, and she wanted the dog to be safe. Meanwhile, there I was, almost eight years old, secretly hating her for taking my dog away."

After her eighth birthday, Lannert started to see a different side of the father she'd always admired. He started off by introducing her to a new game called "touch tongues," which progressed rapidly to more forceful activities like genital touching and oral sex.

At first, Lannert said she didn't mind – it didn't hurt her, and it made her father happy. She admitted that she also liked having a secret that made her feel closer to her beloved Daddy. He was "all I needed," she said. But when she was nine years old, her father's molestation got even more aggressive – he started raping her.

"I felt like he was just tearing me apart," she recalls. "It felt like I was literally being ripped in half, and he was saying such hateful things to me. I didn't know what to do."

She also remembers wondering if all fathers did this to their daughters – but said once he actually started raping her, she could tell "that wasn't right," because it was more violent and painful than the "games" they'd been playing prior to that.

"Any man who can hold his daughter down and rape her is evil," she said. "And nobody stopped him. No one."

Lannert's father told her there was no use tattling to her mom – according to Tom, Deb already knew about what he was doing to their daughter. For Lannert, it felt like a betrayal, and she began to blame her mother for the abuse that her father was forcing on her.

The bitterness Lannert felt toward her mother only intensified when her parents divorced when she was 12 years old.

"I became resentful even more so of my mother for leaving my dad, and almost even took his side in the whole divorce," she said.

She made the decision to continue living with her father when her mother moved out – even though he was still abusing her regularly, anywhere from three to five times each week. To Lannert, the abuse wasn't coming from the same man who she'd been so close to, growing up.

"At some point, I separated my dad into two different people," she said. "My dad, and then Tom, the man who would abuse me."

A deadly misunderstanding

A babysitter finally caught on to Lannert's discomfort, and asked the young girl if her father had been hurting her. When Lannert replied that he was, the babysitter tried to tell Lannert's mother – but Deb didn't think much of it. In fact, years later, she admitted that at the time, she'd thought the babysitter simply meant Lannert had been spanked by her father.

"What I felt was that he loved them and he would not hurt them. I thought he loved his daughters," Deb told ABC News. "I feel like I failed to protect my children ... and I will never ever forget that. I will never live this down no matter what."

In Lannert's memoir, she describes how her maternal grandfather had "fondled" her mother, Deb – and, according to Lannert's account, the sexual abuse going on at her mother's childhood home also "was never acknowledged."

"But because allegations weren't made – the words 'I am being molested' were never spoken – the situation could be quietly ignored," Lannert wrote.

This kind of misunderstanding is part of the reason why Lannert now advocates for victims of sexual abuse – and speaks out about the value of teaching kids what is acceptable and what isn't.

"That's why it's so important to find the real words," she explained. "If we don't name it, people can make it mean what they want it to mean. If you say, 'my father raped me,' they get it. But I didn't even have that word."

Eventually, Lannert couldn't stand it anymore, and made the decision to live with her mother. But her younger sister Christy continued to live with Tom, which made Lannert feel uneasy. Christy had only ever suffered physical abuse at the hands of their father, Lannert said.

"I felt like I was protecting her by taking the sexual abuse," she explained. "If he'd hit her, I'd just thank God that's all it was."

When Christy was in first grade, the beatings began. After her father was killed, she told ABC News that by the time she was 12 years old, Tom was pushing to drink alcohol with him. And, she said, the more he drank, the more violent and abusive his behaviour would

become. Even decades later, she can't handle revisiting the house where she grew up with her older sister.

"I don't care to see the stairs that he used to kick me down," she said. "I don't, I don't want to see the windows that I would have to climb out at night, so I didn't have to wake up being choked."

One day, after Christy called her older sister begging for help, Lannert decided to go back to the house.

"I walked in and opened the door, and there he was," she said, remembering how Tom immediately threw her down and began raping her. "When he got done raping me, he kicked me – and I got smart probably for the first time ever. I was going to fight."

That day, she said, was the last straw. One month later, the two girls snuck into their father's house. Lannert had argued with Tom earlier that day, and the sisters were coming home late at night – hoping their father would already be passed out. They often sneaked in through the window in the basement, Lannert explained.

He was passed out on the couch, but Christy accidentally woke him. He started yelling at her, while Lannert retreated to the basement to grab Tom's gun. By the time she made it back up the stairs, she said, he'd passed out again. Almost without thinking, she shot him in the collarbone – and he sat up immediately.

"All of a sudden, he just started yelling," she said. "I remember thinking, 'he can't get up, because if he gets up, he'll kill us.' So I picked the gun back up and just closed my eyes and pulled the trigger."

Lannert also remembers thinking that Tom "didn't deserve to live," and Christy felt the same way. She told police at the time that she "may have" told her sister to "just do it."

The next day, the girls talked to an adult friend about what they'd done, and the friend helped her get rid of the gun. When she called the police, she told them she'd come home to find her father dead on the sofa – likely killed during a burglary.

Eventually, though, Lannert confessed. She told authorities that she'd killed her father because she "hated him" and that "he needed to die." Christy agreed.

"I had this mind-set, 'this is going to end,'" she explained. "I wanted him to stop. I wanted him to know we're leaving and I can stand up to (him). I didn't ever really make a conscious choice. I guess somewhere in my mind I did, but I wanted him to know that I could fight against him."

She claimed the killing was in self-defense, but prosecutors argued that she hadn't suffered any abuse. In fact, even when police asked Lannert if her father had been abusing her and she told them that he had, no rape-kit test was ever administered. They didn't even ask for more details.

Determining the motive

One officer, though, had her back. Lt. Tom Schulte listened to Lannert's story after she made her confession. She explained to him that the many years of abuse had worn her down, and driven her to commit the crime.

"The last thing I told that young lady when I left her – and it was late that night, I told her, 'I'll be there for you,'" he said.

However, Schulte's testimony didn't support the argument the prosecution was making against Lannert.

The motive for the murder, prosecutors alleged, was money. They accused Lannert of forging his checks and using his credit cards – and said that with Tom out of the picture, Lannert stood to inherit almost $100,000 from her father's estate.

"I had his permission to use the account," Lannert said. "I wasn't working at the time, and he didn't want me working. It was a way of him isolating me."

Many people also questioned Lannert's choice to continue living with her father when her parents' marriage ended, if he was truly an abusive man. But she said that at the time, it was the only option that "made sense" for her.

"We got sent back and forth between the two of them a lot, and there were times that he didn't hurt me," she explained. "My father loved me, not the abuser who would rape me. They weren't (the same person) in my mind."

To Lannert, judging the decision she made as a child who was suffering through tremendous abuse does nothing to help the situation – and can make life even more difficult for the victims of these kinds of crimes.

"A lot of times, we wind up seeing more victimization because of the choices we make," she said. "My life was hell, and I was struggling just to be able to survive every day – and then, after the fact, I have to face answers of why I didn't do this or that. It's harsh."

Lannert also asserts that she did try to leave, moving 7,000 miles away to live with her mother on the island of Guam. But when she received a desperate call from Christy, she couldn't ignore the fact that her sister might need her help.

"All I really cared about was making sure that Christy never had to go through that pain that I had to go through, ever," she said. "I never wanted that for her."

She'd even tried to convince her father to let Christy leave with her, but Tom refused. According to Lannert, all he wanted Christy for was to maintain what little control he still had over his eldest daughter.

Lannert's lawyer tried to argue the defense of insanity or mental defect, attempting to use the "battered spouse syndrome" to explain her behaviour – however, in a pre-trial ruling, the court ordered limited mention of the term.

Still, several expert witnesses were brought in to testify at the trial and conceded that Lannert exhibited signs of abuse. The jury also heard from both Lannert and the babysitter she'd tried to confide in about the ongoing abuse – and, in some states, if a jury believed the allegations of abuse, Lannert's plea of self-defense could have been accepted even though her father had been passed out drunk when she shot him.

But in Missouri, the plea wasn't considered to be valid, since Lannert wasn't in immediate danger when she made the decision to pull the trigger and end her father's life. The prosecution was able to convince the jury, which found Lannert guilty of murder in the first degree. After just a one-week trial, the verdict was read – and, in Missouri, a conviction of murder in the first degree carried a mandatory sentence of life in prison, without the possibility of parole.

"The verdict was absolutely appropriate," said McCulloch. "It's the verdict that should have been returned. She got the sentence that she deserved, and that's where she ought to be."

For her part in the murder, Christy pled guilty to the charge of conspiracy to commit murder and spent two and a half years behind bars.

Despite having spent many years investigating sex crimes, and being the first officer to question Lannert after her father's murder, Schulte was never called to testify. Lannert admitted that she felt abandoned and betrayed for many years, until she learned that he would have testified on her behalf, had he been given the opportunity.

Once Lannert was in prison, Schulte said he made the decision not to contact her and explain what had happened. Any contact between them, he believed, would risk calling into question his affidavit – which noted all his observations from the night he had interviewed her.

Several members of the jury also came forward after Lannert had been sentenced, outraged that they hadn't been presented with all of the facts regarding the sexual and physical abuse Lannert had suffered at the hands of her father. A statement was issued by the United States Court of Appeals for the Eight Circuit after Lannert filed a petition for appeal, claiming that the Missouri self-defense statute indicates no specific time frame in which an act of self-defense can occur, following an initial act of aggression or provocation.

"It is therefore deeply troubling that the jury was not completely informed of the scope of the abuse Lannert suffered, her fear, or her rage that her sister may also have been victimized by their father," the statement read. "This evidence of battered spouse syndrome might have placed Lannert's actions in proper context, and may have allowed a jury to conclude that Lannert was not the initial aggressor on the night of her father's death, potentially resulting in a very different outcome than what she faces today."

Still, the court refused to accept Lannert's argument that "a man who raped his daughter, when she was in the third grade, made him 'the initial aggressor,' and the author of his own doom." It also determined that battered spouse syndrome cannot be considered a defense in itself, but rather indicates support for a claim of self-defense.

Released by the grace of God

After exhausting her appeals, Lannert petitioned the court for clemency for years. The affidavit from Schulte was a key part of the request. Her lawyers finally launched a publicity campaign on her behalf, which allowed Lannert to share her story to influential figures like Montel Williams, Nancy Grace, and Oprah Winfrey.

"Having to go public was the worst moment for me," Lannert recalled. "It was so shameful. How was I going to be able to look anybody in the eye again? But then I did it, and I started receiving letters from so many people, saying 'you could have been me.'"

Lannert had spent 18 years in prison before Missouri Governor Matt Blunt looked at her file. In January of 2009, Blunt commuted Lannert's life sentence to twenty years after undertaking an "extensive review of the evidence" – finally, after almost two decades of incarceration, Lannert was free.

"(I was released) by the grace of God and the perseverance of two wonderful attorneys, a police detective who never gave up, and a governor who had a lot of courage," she said.

However, St. Louis County prosecutor Bob McCulloch, who persuaded the court that Lannert was a manipulative liar who killed her father solely for financial reasons, maintained that she deserved to spend the rest of her life behind bars.

"I have not changed my mind at all about Stacey Lannert. She murdered her father for his inheritance, and solely for his inheritance," he told ABC News in March of 2009. "She was never sexually abused by her father or anyone else, and she ought to be back in the penitentiary, and shame on Governor Blunt for letting her out."

According to McCulloch, Tom Lannert was a "bad father" and a "bad drunk" – not a rapist. He claimed Lannert was "lying through her teeth," and that there was no evidence to support her allegations that she had been sexually abused.

"The only credible evidence of any sort of motive is that she did it for the money," he said. "And she's not going to get her hands on it unless she – unless she takes out her father."

To this day, Lannert denies McCulloch's allegations that she "spent wildly" and was only interested in the $500,000 estate that she stood to inherit in the case of her father's death.

"I wanted him to leave me alone; I wanted him to leave her alone," she said. "I didn't really necessarily want him to die, but I didn't want him to be able to... hurt us again, to be able to get us."

Throughout her time in prison, Lannert said it was her own dedication to her faith that kept her patient – even during harder times. Although she worked hard at maintaining a positive attitude, she admitted it was difficult.

"There were times I gave up," she recalled. "I really believed I would spend the rest of my life in prison."

While Lannert agrees that since she did "break one of society's rules," her time in prison was well-deserved – but she said she felt she had no other way of escaping her father's incessant abuse.

"There was nowhere to run to – I didn't feel like there was anywhere I could go that he couldn't find me," she said. "He would tell us how he would find us: the car was registered in his name, he could track me through the social security card number, and he would tell me how he would find me and I believed him."

Since her release from prison, Lannert has founded Healing Sisters, a non-profit organization and resource website dedicated to help women who have suffered abuse. She hopes her work will someday help to end sexual abuse in America.

"Secrets lose their power when they're shared," she explained. "I think that every woman who's been abused thinks at one point in time, 'I'm going to kill you.' There's power in the thought – but not in the actual act itself, and I don't think people understand that. Now, not only do I have the shame and guilt of what he did to me, I also have the shame and guilt of my actions."

She also now recognizes that a more powerful action would have been to turn her father in – to put him "in the defendant's seat," she said, "and make my accusations against him."

"I was free in my heart."

Still, during her time in prison, Lannert was able to do some healing – and was finally able to deal with what her father put her through for all those years. While she said she's certainly pleased to be out, prison made her confront many of the uncomfortable feelings she had been pushing down.

"I couldn't run away from my past at all," she said. "The compassion and encouragement and support that I have been met with from other women who went through the same thing just really made me feel like I wasn't alone."

She also kept herself busy in prison by investing her time in a positive hobby – learning to train dogs to help people with disabilities. When she was finally released, she met up with Schulte in St. Louis – and he asked her to train his dog.

"I feel a connection with him that I'll probably never feel with another human being, because he was the first person who helped me, who believed me," she said. "It took a long time for it to come to fruition, but he did stand behind me and helped. And I'm just very thankful."

With some closure on the situation, Lannert said she can now see that Tom, her abuser, and the father she loved were the same person all along.

"I had to, in order to forgive myself for the action that I took, because there were moments that I missed my father," she admitted. "I had to forgive him in order to be able to forgive myself – but there's a difference between forgiving and forgetting."

Forgiving, she said, gave her the ability to move past what she has endured, and finally look toward the future.

"If I don't forgive him, then I'm in prison – it might not be a physical prison, but it's psychological prison," she said. "You know, I was incarcerated, and I was free in my heart. The rest was geography."

Although she felt free in her heart, it's nothing compared to the true freedom of being released from prison. Adjusting to life outside of jail has been challenging, as Lannert said she's not used to being able to do whatever she wants, whenever she wants.

"I ask for permission all the time," she said. "I need to learn how to break that. It doesn't seem real to me yet. But I'm working on it, and I'm so happy. I can't believe I got this second chance at life, so I'm just excited."

While Lannert knows some people still won't believe her story, or might judge her for how she dealt with her father's abuse, she said she chooses not to hold it against them.

"Every person in America is entitled to their own opinion," she stated. "I can't judge them."

HUSBAND KILLER : THE TRUE STORY OF TRACEY GRISSOM

58

SARAH CAMDEN

Claiming to be a victim of rape and other abuses, a distraught Tracey Grissom would travel to her ex-husband Hunter's workplace and shoot him six times in the back, receiving a twenty-five-year life sentence for his murder.

Her defense attorney would argue that Tracey was motivated by post-traumatic stress disorder caused by her Hunter's constant abuse and sexual assaults. One jury member had even asked the judge to be lenient in her sentencing as they were not allowed to hear details of her Hunter's alleged abuses (beatings, rape, sodomy).

But what really happened in the years that led up to May 15th, 2012? Was she in fact the victim of years of abuse by a psychotic husband? Or did she want to cash in on his $100,000 life insurance policy?

INSTANT ATTRACTION

The couple would meet during a dinner party in 2003 in Tuscaloosa, Alabama. Tracey was twenty-one years old and going through a divorce. She had a son, James Michael, from the previous marriage.

Family and friends would describe the union as "love at first sight." Hunter was blown away by the young Tracey's blue eyes and facial beauty.

"For him, it was love at first sight," crime author William Phelps said. "She was gorgeous."

A whirlwind courtship would ensue and the couple would elope in 2004.

"In the beginning, it was good," Tracey told CBS' 48 hours. "We had a friendship. Just your normal, honeymoon phase marriage."

"He was fun," Tracey said. "And he was attractive."

Hunter was two years younger than Tracey, however, and his mother felt that he had jumped the gun too early in the relationship.

Her words proved to be prophetic as after only eight months into the marriage, the marriage went south.

According to Tracey, their marital problems began with Hunter's drug addiction.

"I had caught him smoking marijuana," Tracey said. "Doing illegal things could cause a problem and I couldn't risk losing my son over."

Tracey claimed that she threatened her new spouse with a divorce but Hunter gave her his word that he would stop with his drug use. She stated that the relationship improved and the decided to start a construction company together.

"I took out an equity line to start a company," Tracey said. "Which was Grissom Construction. It was all in my name."

Hunter specialized in building elaborate boat docks. He had an artistic eye and could do docks, stairs, and other accouterments. The business began to grow in short order.

"They're going to take on the world," Phelps said. "They're going to be entrepreneurs and they're gonna make it."

They then had a daughter of their own, Anna Grace. The child was a long time coming for the couple. They had been trying for a long time as Tracey had five miscarriages before Anna Grace was born.

"She was premature," Tracey recalled. "Her heart and lungs were not developed. A very stressful time."

Behind closed doors things were rocky. On the surface, however, things looked good. They had a young family and were making money.

"All-American family," Phelps said. "White-picket fence. The whole nine yards. Middle-class. Suburbia. Maybe the Prince Charming that she's been waiting for."

But again, this was only on the surface. Tracey harbored secrets of her own. One of which was her own addiction to prescription drugs.

"Psychologically, there's something going on here," Phelps said. "There's something going on behind those beautiful eyes and it ain't good."

Tracey would often turn on on the children, showing off her temper. Then she would turn on Hunter.

"This would cause friction in the marriage," Phelps said. "And where there's friction, there's fire."

SETTING THE STAGE

Tracey would later state that Hunter would "act strangely" shortly before she filed divorce. She was a registered nurse and gave him an over-the-counter drug test. According to her, Hunter tested posted for marijuana, Oxycontin, opiates, and methamphetamine.

Hunter would later be arrested for marijuana possession but his family would insist that he never did the harder drugs.

Tracey would file for divorce in the summer of 2010 after six years of marriage. According to her, this would prompt physical abuse from Hunter.

Hunter had to move out but their divorce agreement would allow him access to the home.

"In September of 2010," Tracey recalled. "That was the first time he physically hit me. It (the abuse) got progressively worse. He had made the comments that if I told anybody he would kill me. I believed him."

Hunter' co-workers and family members would have a different take on the situation, however. His co-workers remembered a time when she tracked him down at one of the jobs and made a scene.

"She's screaming, jumping on him," Hunter's co-worker said. "Said something about him having another girlfriend and used the expression about, 'You are mine. I'll kill you. I'll kill you. You are mine."

"She's borderline demonic," Hunter's mother said. " mean, I absolutely believe—that she is that troubled."

Hunter's family continued to believe that he did not abuse Tracey.

"He did not have an abusive, an angry bone in his body," Hunter's aunt Gina said. "In fact, we kind of laughed at him because he was too laid-back."

The divorce was finalized in October of 2010.

EVIDENCE OF ABUSE?

Loran Richards was the first of Tracey's friends to notice the minor injuries on her body. She would inquire about the bruises but the answers she received were always evasive. Seeing Tracey with a black eye, however, forced her to try and get more answers.

"I said, Tracey, you may have terrible luck," Richards recalled. "But nobody is so unlucky that they trip, fall down the stairs, and hit their face on a baseball in the eye socket. So don't give me a lame excuse. You don't have to give me any excuse, but let's take a picture."

Tracey broke down. She gave her friend all of the grisly details, detailing the abuse she suffered at the hands of Hunter. Loran then became her advocate, taking pictures of Tracey's injuries. She would later state that she saw blood stains and other signs of abuse at Tracey's home.

THAT FATEFUL NIGHT

Now divorced, Hunter would arrive at Tracey's home on November 22nd, 2010.

According to Tracey, he then became enraged when Tracey told him that she had spent the night with a new lover.

"He told me that he was gonna kill me," Tracey recalled. Tracey stated that she tried to escape, running into the closet in order to "get away from the kids and to pray." Tracey's eleven-year-old son from a previous relationship was in the home as was the four-year-old daughter they have together.

Hunter caught up with her and knocked her to the ground. He tied a belt around her ankles and then began choking her.

Half-conscious, Tracey alleged to have been raped and sodomized.

The brutal attack would leave Tracey unconscious. She would wake up the next morning on the bathroom floor.

"I called Hunter," Tracey recalled. "I told him that I was bleeding and that I was hurt and that I needed help. And he told me, 'Fuck you. I hope you die.'"

Tracey wound up in the emergency room after the attack. Hospital records would show that she had a laceration on her head, bruises, and ligature marks on her feet.

Tracey would then be referred to the Turning Point domestic violence center.

Marian Waters would describe Tracey's injuries as among the worst she had ever seen in a twenty-year career.

Waters would testify that Tracey had suffered a horrific assault. She described her mental state as typical of someone who had just been raped; fearful, jumpy, fearing for her life.

Tracey had suffered a hematoma on her side that was the side of a grapefruit. She also claimed to have experienced rectal nerve damage which would require surgery as well as torn vaginal muscles requiring her to have a hysterectomy.

Police were called and Hunter would be arrested for rape, sodomy, kidnapping and domestic violence.

"And at that point, I feared for my life," Tracey recalled. "And I feared for my children's life."

A HIDDEN AGENDA

Hunter would be freed on bail but Tracey got a restraining order against him. She bought a gun and did not go anywhere unarmed.

She took photos of her injuries on the night of the alleged attack and texted them to Loran. Later, they would take more pictures.

Angered, Hunter would stop paying her spousal and child support. Tracey, however, may have had another scenario in mind for obtaining money.

She had forced Hunter to take out a $103,000 life insurance policy around the time their daughter was born.

On May 24, 2012, the day before Tracey shot Hunter, she would place a call to MetLife that was recorded.

"Thank you for calling MetLife, this is Pam. May I please have your name?"

"Tracey Grissom."

Tracey would then explain that she was angry that her husband stopped making payments on his policy. During their divorce proceedings, he had agreed to continue paying the premiums. Tracey stated she was calling to make sure that they had the correct address on file.

"Is there anything else I can do for you today?

"That's gonna be it!" Tracey said, hanging up.

"Well, May 14th was just like any other day," Tracey said, explaining the call to the insurance company. "However, I had moved four different times. Me and my children were running. We were running from Hunter. So I had called the company to let them know that they had my old address and to make an address change."

FALSE RAPE?

Shelly Standridge was hired by Hunter to defend him in the rape case. She would state that Hunter denied raping or even assaulting Tracey that night. Hunter did, however, admit to the fact that he and his wife had consensual sex that night...Rough consensual sex.

"So that night," Standridge said. "Hunter said that she was depressed and claiming she was going to kill herself. She was saying she wanted their relationship to work."

So she undressed in front of him. Her beauty was always impossible for Hunter to resist.

The two had sex despite Hunter having a new girlfriend at home.

Hunter's aunt, Gina, believed that Tracey wanted to kill Hunter before the rape case went to court.

"He had a new girlfriend, he was living with her," Phelps said. "He was moving on with his life. Hunter would claim that Tracey was jealous, obsessive, even stalked them."

"Hunter had moved on," Hunter's aunt said. "There was some court dates coming up that would prove that Hunter was innocent. There were court dates coming up that he would get visitation to his daughter. She had a lot to lose."

Tracey was on the anti-anxiety drug Klonopin. Hunter would tell his attorney that Tracey would take more than her prescribed dose. Because of this, she fell and cut her head. Hunter would then leave the house around 10:30 pm and go to his father's house. Tracey would call him hours later, at 3:20 am.

Hunter would state that Tracey had called to threaten him. She told him if he didn't want the responsibility of the children then she would make it where he would never be able to see them again.

Hunter's attorney did not know what Tracey's motive was for crying rape. She was very upset that he had a girlfriend.

MORE LIES...

Hunter would be arrested nearly twelve hours later, to his total shock.

Tracey would give her side of the story to the police which later is proven to be false.

She would tell police that Hunter had thrown her against the bathtub around 10 pm and claim to be unconscious until 4 am the next morning.

"But her phone records show she was on the phone all night, so she was never unconscious," Standridge said. "She was also using her data at 10:42 that night. She was using it again at 10:50 that night. ... She sends a text to her boyfriend at 1:49 am. She sends a text to her friend at 2:07 am. She sends another text to her boyfriend at 2:07 am."

Tracey would blame the calls on Hunter.

"All I do know is I was not the only person using my phone that night," Tracey said, suggesting that Hunter used her phone.

Medical records would show that Tracey's head wound was "purely superficial".

Only one suture was needed.

Furthermore, there was nothing on the medical record to support the fact that Tracey experienced vaginal and rectal tears. She did have bruises on her ankle and legs but the photos taken by police at the emergency room would not resemble the same photos that Tracey and her friend Loran would take days later. In the photos taken at the emergency room, an area of Tracey's body has no bruises. Days later, there is discoloration.

Tracey's attorney would blame the discrepancy on "blood thinners" which would cause Tracey to bruise easily.

There was also a discrepancy in her phone records. She would take a photo of her inner thigh, a deep bruise. This area of her body was not photographed by police during her emergency room visit. But on December 9th, almost two weeks later, Tracey took a photo of her inner thigh with the deep bruise

"He (Hunter) told me that he would make it to where nobody would ever want me," Tracey said after a 2010 attack. "I didn't report it because I thought he would kill me."

THE FINAL STRAW

Tracey woke up pissed on May 15th, 2012.

Hunter had been ordered to pay $2,100 a month for the rest of his life. He was not complying with the court order claiming that he was "out of work."

Tracey stated that she was on her way to a job interview when she saw a Grissom Construction sign out of the corner of her eye.

She stated that her initial plan was to take a photograph of Hunter at the job site in order to show proof that he was working as part of her litigation.

"I was getting ready to take the picture and when I looked up he was standing almost directly towards the front of the boat trailer," Tracey said. "He was looking back directly at me. He had this face, that's like mean - just, I don't know how to describe it. I mean, I see it over and over like it's right there all the time. He flipped me the bird, which to me was kinda like, 'Yeah I'm workin. Screw you.' And at that point, I panicked. At that point, I didn't know what else to do except to defend myself."

Tracey started firing. The first shot hit Hunter in the arm. He started to run and she fired again repeatedly. One of the bullets punctured Hunter's heart and he died of massive internal bleeding.

William Dockery was working with Hunter and was an eyewitness to the shooting. Hunter had turned to Dockery before the shooting and told him to "call the law". Before Dockery could pick up his cell phone, Tracey had commenced shooting.

Tracey then pulled out her own cell phone and called the cops on herself. She tearfully described that she had just murdered her husband.

CONFESSION

Tracey told detectives exactly what was going through her mind when she came upon Hunter at the construction site.

"Tell me about what happened," the detective said. "What led up to...what's going on."

"In November of 2010, he beat me unconscious and raped me...and, and left me for dead....and, and I finally pressed charges against him and he told me that he would make my life a living hell...and that's what he's done."

"What, what happened this morning that led up to you going..."

"I was going to work and I saw him...and he's been claiming that he-he's not working. And, so I pulled in there to take a picture of him...cause it was the truck that's still in my name...and the boat that's still in my name...and the trailer that's still in my name...He just stared at me and flipped me off...and I just went in there and shot him...I just shot him, I shot him, and I shot him."

Tracey would be distraught and tearful during her interrogation room confession. A few weeks later, however, she would call the insurance company to let them know that Hunter had died.

"Well, I was actually calling because I didn't know what I needed to do ... Hunter passed away May 15th and I actually am going a court case right now because it was due to self-defense..."

Hunter's family went ballistic over this. Tracey would claim that she had no money but she continued to pay his life insurance premiums.

"Even through the times when she's screamin' that she's destitute and has no money ... she continued to pay life insurance premium," Hunter's mother said.

"I don't think my sister concocted a story," Tracey's sister said. "Just so she could get insurance money. ... But that's all they (the prosecution) had."

THE TRIAL

Tracey's allegations of rape and sodomy would not be allowed in court testimony. She was allowed, however, to detail the effects of Hunter's abuse on her were.

Taking the stand, Tracey would lift up her shirt in court and show herself wearing a colostomy bag. She stated that she had undergone several surgeries after her husband's daily rapes wherein she suffered permanent rectal and vaginal damage.

Hunter's family was then allowed to speak at the hearing.

"This tremendous loss has changed me," Hunter's mother, Melanie Garner said. "And I don't know how to change back."

Chloe, Hunter's sister, had a victim's services officer read her letter in court.

"Tracey is psychotic," Chloe wrote. "She is the most selfish person human being on this earth."

"Every mother should pray every night that your son doesn't fall in love with someone like Tracey," Hunter's aunt, Gina Grissom said. "There have been lots of allegations against Hunter. We've never believed anything that has come out of her (Tracey's) mouth."

His aunt then looked directly at Tracey.

"Hunter was proud of his name. Why would you still choose to use our name, and bring it down?" suggesting that if Tracey hated him so much why didn't she go revert to her maiden name after the divorce.

The jurors would find Tracey guilty of murder. She would be sentenced to twenty-five years in prison.

One of the jurors, Janice Kelly, would contact Grissom's attorney Warren Freeman the morning after the trial. She had remorse over her decision and said that she wouldn't have convicted her had they had the rapes and abuse allegations been introduced as evidence.

"I feel I made a mistake," Kelly said. "If I had to do it over again, we'd have had a hung jury. We didn't get her side. She did not get a fair trial."

"We voted to convict because there was no dispute that Tracey shot Hunter," the jury foreman wrote in a letter that was addressed in the courthouse. "Jurors didn't believe prosecutor claims that she did it in order to collect a life insurance policy. We felt the shooting was a crime of passion, not for financial gain and that she should be sentenced accordingly. I wish we had seen evidence of the rape allegation. We feel that she just 'lost it.'"

"It's not fair, it's not fair!" Tracey sobbed as she was led out of the courthouse and to jail.

"We think the sentencing was too harsh," Tracey's attorney Warren Freeman said. "Considering you have the foreperson of the jury actually saying, we don't feel like she should be punished according to being found guilty of murder. Let's just say that there will be a basis for a new trial, and part of it will be something that the jurors saw that they weren't supposed to see and I'm going to just leave it at that until I file my motion."

"My son died running for his life," Hunter's mother said. "I don't know what was running through his mind but I hear him say 'momma.'"

"People who think that I murdered him in cold blood," Tracey said. "Either don't know the whole story or don't know everything that's happened.

Tracey was asked on CBS' 48 hours if she regretted pulling the trigger on that fateful day.

"No," she said flatly. "Because if I hadn't I would be dead. I truly believe that."

"She has a way of making everything she does look right," Hunter's aunt, Gina scoffed.

AMBER CUMMINGS

On the surface, James and Amber Cummings had it all.

They had been married for twelve years. James had inherited millions of dollars from his father and they owned a home in the peaceful, seaside town of Belfast, Maine.

"On paper, they were a couple that looked as if they had everything," forensic psychologist Paula Orange said. "Definitely one of those cases where looks are more than deceiving. They are downright deadly."

The couple met in Fort Bragg, California. Amber was a tall brunette while James was overweight and had an awkward vibe about him.

Amber found him charming, however, and would later describe him as the "nicest guy she'd ever met." She would marry him at 19 years of age and things looked bright for the young couple until Amber got pregnant.

"That is when his personality started to change," Orange said. "He would drive away Amber's family members in California and seek to keep her isolated. This brought much consternation to Amber's side of the family, obviously. There was one heart-breaking instance where Amber's mother and sister went to a neighbor's yard just to get a glimpse of Amber's daughter riding her tricycle."

James wanted no outside influence on Amber or their daughter so he began moving the family around. They left California when Amber turned five and moved to Texas. Then they traveled the country in a motor home until 2007 when the finally settled in Belfast, Maine.

"My husband said that he hated people and that he didn't care where we moved," Amber said. "I always wanted to live in a nice, small town in Maine."

EARLY LIFE

James' life seemed to have been one of trouble even though he was born into wealth.

His father would be murdered by one of his former employees in 1997 which was preceded by James making headline news as he videotaped his own mother doing heroin.

James would have numerous run-ins with the law himself.

"He had a bunch of assault charges," Orange said. "Some were cases where he was the victim. Others were cases where he was the perpetrator. When he was the perp, his father's money always bailed him out."

According to some Internet rumors, James' father had allegedly injured himself while getting off a forklift on one of the docks in the Fort Bragg harbor, breaking his knee in the fall.

Cummings then went to a friend's house and fell to the ground outside claiming that he "tripped in a hole." James' father then sued the owners of the property and won.

"That gives you an idea of the kind of guy James' father was," Orange said. "Rumors abound on the internet and in the Fort Bragg community about how he acquired his wealth. None of it is verifiable aside from the fact that the majority of the trust is funneled through a trailer park, which is odd."

Cummings Sr. would own many businesses and it would be one of his employees, a man named Williams Vargas who would gun him down.

Vargas detonated a homemade bomb he called a "firecracker" outside Cummings' home. The disgruntled employee then panicked as one of Cummings' neighbors drove by and blocked his escape. Cummings Sr. then came out with his own gun to investigate the blast which shattered his window.

Vargas then pulled out his own gun and shot Cummings. He had been working for Cummings at the Noyo Harbor trailer park and was allowed to live there in exchange for labor. But he began having problems with other residents which he would blame Cummings Sr. for.

Cummings, 77 years old at the time of his murder, had built his wealth by running restaurants, motels, a fish-processing plant as well as trailer parks. He also owned the Depot Mall shopping center and a McDonald's restaurant.

``Jim was quite an entrepreneur. He had quite a lot of land holdings, in some key areas, really, in the harbor and other areas around," former City Manager Gary Milliman said.

James Jr. would be the beneficiary of his father's death. He would tell people that he made his living "selling off Texas real estate" but the truth was that he was a trust fund kid living off the businesses that his father created.

The trust fund started off by giving Jams a whopping ten million dollars a year. The funds would deplete rapidly, however, as James would have a six-year legal battle against trustees whom he thought were mismanaging the money.

His mental illness would grow worse as his finances decreased.

NEO-NAZI SYMPATHIES

"He would go on daily rants about Barack Obama," Orange said. "Which would seem harmless at first until Amber realized that James was, in fact, a white supremacist. He began spending his days hunting down rare Nazi artifacts on the Internet and purchasing them."

James had applied to the National Socialist Movement, one of the largest neo-Nazi clubs in the country. He had written numerous white supremacy organizations on-line and began to mix toxic chemicals in their kitchen sink while telling Amber about his desire to make a "dirty bomb."

James had hired a pair of contractors to paint the interior of the house. The painters would later testify to witnessing James berate his wife. He would tell the men about his guns and go on about Adolf Hitler.

Thinking he had an eager audience, James bragged about his collection of silverware and plate settings that he claimed to have been used by Hitler himself.

"Check this out," James showed a swastika flag to the painter. "This was real. Not a knock-off. They actually waved this same flag while Hitler spoke."

James would run his household as if he were Hitler himself, marching around the home wearing a black hat and uniform with a Nazi armband.

Working himself up into a Nazi-like frenzy of rage, he would then abuse Amber physically, emotionally and sexually.

"He stripped away whatever self-esteem she had," Orange said. "He had no friends himself and didn't allow her to have any either."

As the years went by, James developed paranoid schizophrenic tendencies which had given birth to ideas that grew more bizarre with time. The married couple slept in separate bedrooms and James had guns placed under both of their pillows "just in case."

On one occasion, Amber left the home for an extended period of time. James immediately became enraged upon her arrival back. He demanded to know where she was and who she was with. Amber had gone to meet with a home-schooling group which they both previously agreed would be a good idea.

James went ballistic, berating Amber and throwing his sharpened Nazi knives against the wall.

CHILD ABUSE

James did not limit his abuse to Amber. His paranoid anger soon extended to their daughter, Clara.

This became evident to Amber when their daughter had come across James' collection of Nazi knives and began examining them.

"Leave those alone!" James screamed as he ran into the room and grabbed the box of knives away from the girl. "These belonged to the Führer! The Führer!"

Amber had very little self-esteem left, but she intervened when James would physically abuse their daughter. She would throw herself between the two and take the beating herself.

This would only incite James further as the would beat Amber then march up to Clara's room and continue his abuse.

"He kept them isolated and feeling helpless," Orange said. "They tried to escape on a few occasions but he caught them, keeping them locked in the house. She thought he had some kind of superhuman power."

CHILD PORNOGRAPHY

Seeking new outlets, James' mind became so perverted that he soon began indulging in child pornography. He showed his collection to Amber who shuddered in horror.

"Which one do you like best?" he would ask his wife, pointing to a series of pictures on the scream.

In addition to the child pornography, James began teaching his daughter to see the world through his racist viewpoint.

"This is equal-opportunity hatred," he preached to his daughter. "We can hate everybody."

"He was deluded," Orange said. "He actually saw himself as the second coming of Hitler. He began seeing his daughter as his future helper, someone who would be in charge of 'reconditioning' women and children after he declared war on the United States."

James wanted to build a torture chamber in the basement of the house. He told Amber about his desire to kill people and "peel the skin off their bones." He also obsessed on the Showtime television series, "Dexter", which featured a serial killer as the protagonist. James would then take long walks around the Belfast area, daydreaming about living out his 'Dexter' fantasy.

"He constantly talked about the different ways of killing and torturing people and hiding their bodies," Amber said. "He used to say it was a need in him."

THE FINAL STRAW

"The abuse happened incrementally for her," Orange said. "It is easy to sit back and judge a person like her, saying that she should have just left. But she was like a frog in a pot of cool water before it starts to boil. The abuse started small at first then bit by bit it increased as her self-esteem diminished. But when it came to protecting her daughter, she had to act."

One December 9th, 2008, Amber Cummings finally had enough.

She got up like she normally did after another night of abuse by her husband.

"Amber discovered James messing around with the chemicals in the kitchen," Orange said. "He said that he would bury her in the backyard if he said anything."

She sent her daughter downstairs to eat breakfast while she pulled out a .45 caliber pistol from underneath her pillow.

Then she held the gun underneath her own throat.

"Amber's first thought was to kill herself," Orange said. "But then she saw her daughter's doll in the room. She shuddered to think of her daughter spending the rest of her childhood with her father as she realized that it was only a matter of time before James' obsession with child pornography would make him do something to Clara. So she had to seek an alternative course of action."

Amber would later tell court-appointed psychologists that James' infatuation with child pornography and his "sexual attraction to young girls" made her believe that he was becoming obsessed with their daughter.

Fueled by her protective maternal instinct, Amber entered the bedroom where James was sleeping. She never had any gumption to stand up for herself when James abused her.

But when it came to protecting her daughter, a whole new Amber showed up.

She pointed the gun at the back of James' head and fired. Blood splattered against the bedpost. Shocked by her own display of violence, Amber sprinted down the steps and ordered her daughter to go to her neighbor's and stay there.

"If it wasn't for my daughter, I would have committed suicide years ago," Amber said. "Some of the mental torture will never leave me the rest of my life. It was so severe, it will be with me every day."

Amber then called the police and told them what she did.

"It's hard for us to justify shooting somebody who's asleep in the bed," Sheriff Jeffrey Trafton said. "But when we arrived she looked more like a victim than a killer."

"She was in a state of shock," Orange said. "She had finally taken action to free herself from years of abuse. The state, of course, cannot let such a deed go unchecked."

A CONSPIRACY AFOOT?

As police investigated the murder scene, they discovered another James Cummings secret.

He was gathering materials to make a "dirty bomb."

Fueled by his white supremacist ideology, James planned to go to Washington, D.C for Barack Obama's presidential inauguration. Once there, he would set off his dirty bomb.

"He had all the ingredients inside the garage," Orange said. "The FBI found the instructions for the dirty bomb. There were four 1-gallon containers with uranium, thorium and beryllium powder. There were numerous other jugs which contained lithium metal, thermite, magnesium ribbon, black iron oxide and other explosive substances. James Cummings meant business and there is clear evidence he was going to follow through on his plan. Whether he could have pulled it off is another story."

Had his plan gone to fruition, James could have potentially killed hundreds of people.

Amber saved not only herself but innumerable lives by killing James herself.

"The stuff that he had wasn't dangerous," Bangor Police Chief Jeffrey Trafton said. "In its present form, it wasn't dangerous to the community. Technicians told me what you had to do, you had to get real close for a long period of time before it would have any effect as far as the radioactivity. When the stuff was found, obviously detectives from the state police came and we didn't know what it was. But there was no danger to the community. That was established fairly quickly. But my involvement since it was handed over to the state police has been little to none."

THE TRIAL

Amber would remain in a state of shock after the murder. She worried more about her daughter's well-being than her own. She was fully prepared to go to jail.

"Her mental state was still askew after she killed James," Orange said. "She probably saw prison as a welcome respite from her abusive life. She had been in 'prison' already and saw the jail system as a safe place."

Amber would plead guilty during trial proceedings. Her story would make the media rounds, however, and she soon found numerous supporters in her small Maine town. People showed up wearing "Free Amber" t-shirts.

"There was no way in hell a jury in that vicinity would have found her guilty," Orange said. "None."

Amber seemed to have found leniency on both sides of the judicial system. Her attorney and the prosecutors would come up with a plea deal which called for a sentence of up to eight years but with Amber serving no less than a year. This would be followed by six years of probation.

Her attorney then recommended to the judge that Amber spend no whatsoever behind bars while the Assistant Attorney General, Leane Zania, wanted Cummings to spend a year in jail.

"This kind of 'self-help' is severely anti-social behavior," Zania wrote. "It will be punished accordingly."

During the course of the trial, Amber would not take the stand in her defense. Three mental health experts who had counseled her after the killing all affirmed the fact that Amber had endured traumatic abuse. They advised the judge not to send her to jail.

The psychiatrists had given Amber a diagnosis of "shared psychotic disorder" which in layman's terms meant that she had absorbed some of his craziness just by being around him.

"You don't hang out by the outhouse without getting a rash," Orange said. "So that is how Amber was able to endure all of that psychological trauma. She became so desensitized to it that it became the norm after a few years."

The judge sentenced her to eight years in prison but it was a suspended sentence, allowing her to go free.

"The terrible thing is, I was forced to take the life of someone that I loved very much to save my daughter that I love very much," Amber said. "It's something that I will have to live with for the rest of my life, and it won't be easy. I'll always wonder. I'll always be looking over my shoulder, always wondering if he can come back from the dead."

In her public remarks, Amber requested that the community forgive her husband and not have any anger toward him.

"I just want to thank the community and people of Maine," Amber said after leaving the courtroom. "Because without them, I don't think my daughter and I could have made all this progress. Really, really wonderful caring people. If I was anywhere else, we wouldn't be doing this well. I believe that with all my heart."

"The people around here are pretty incredible. They gave me the benefit of the doubt, and a chance to prove myself. There was a lot of support, an unbelievable amount of support, in Belfast. People came out and took care of us and made sure we had everything we need."

Amber stated that after she shot James that she fell into a "state of shock and numbness." She would continue to dream about James, having nightmares about him choking her.

Since then, she dedicated herself to trying to undo the mental damage James did to her daughter.

"I hope to raise a really good kid, who cares a lot about people," Amber said. I hope she ends up strong and can take care of herself. I think she will."

DEATH ROW GRANNY

It never ends.

No way.

No way am I letting this man demean and degrade me another day.

He's just like my father.

A binge drinker. And the binges were happening more and more.

He's on the road to nowhere and taking me with him.

It never ends.

First my father. Now him.

Fuck it.

I threw the cigarette on the blanket. I knew it was flammable.

Then I watched the smoke rise and smiled.

In Lumberton, North Carolina, Thomas Burke fell victim to a house fire which was caused by a burning cigarette. Investigative authorities thought that he had fallen asleep while smoking, leaving thirty-eight-year-old Velma Burke as his widow.

They didn't know that the fire was set by Velma.

Velma knew how to play the part of the grieving widow. She cried and gave the authorities the requisite crocodile tears. No one would believe that the murder of Thomas Burke would set off a series of killings performed by the seemingly kind and harmless church-going woman with the soft voice.

EARLY LIFE

Velma Bullard grew up as the second of nine children in the rural part of Sampson County, North Carolina.

Times were tough for the Bullard family. They would live on a small farm with no electricity, running water or an outhouse.

"They had to go outdoors," forensic psychologist Paula Orange said. "The entire family had to endure the indignity of going into the woods or using pots to shit and piss."

The home was small and cramped for the nine children. Velma would be forced to sleep in the same bedroom with her parents until the age of five.

Her father was a loom repairman (fixing an apparatus that was used to weave clothing) and an abusive alcoholic. Velma had an older brother, Olive, who were subject to his nightly beatings. Lillie, her mother, was too meek to protect her children from her husband's violent outbursts.

"She had the type of father who would not need any provocation," Orange said. "He would take out the pettiest frustrations, like not being able to find something around the house, and take it out on the children. Velma would become resentful toward her mother who was too weak or indifferent to stop her father from beating on the kids. She accepted his discipline as 'the way it was.'"

Velma would find school as a welcome escape from her dreadful home life. She loved her teacher and was an excellent student during her early grade school years. When she would return home from school, she took solace in the fact that her father would always arrive home late as he worked long hours at the textile mill.

"Her father Murphy had that Protestant work ethic in him," Orange said. "He accepted the long hours and low pay, seeing a kind of nobility in that. Only problem was, he would binge drink. Not store bought alcohol but homemade moonshine. After a couple of shots, he would be 'lit' and inflict his wrath on everyone in the house."

By the age of eleven, Velma would be forced to take on various chores around the farm. She would clean up the house, washing and iron everyone's clothing (eleven people). Her father would chastise her for not mending or sewing his work clothes properly as well.

"Her father was a stern taskmaster," Orange said. "Hell, you can say 'slave driver.' He would have Velma come home early from school days when the laundry got too backed up. Velma hated this and felt embarrassed. Her family didn't have much and as she grew older her classmates began to see her for what she was, a poor girl that was an easy mark for teasing."

Velma would grow to be 5'3" but gain weight as she got older. She would be mocked about her obesity, her shoddy clothes the gap between her two front teeth. She would also be called "knot head" after she ran head first into a boy at school which left a permanent contusion on her forehead.

By the age of twelve, Velma seemed to have taken on all of her mother's duties. She would cook all of the family meals in addition to performing cleaning around the farm house. She would miss school for days at a time as her father forced her to complete chores around the home before she could continue her education.

"Academic achievement was not at the forefront of her father's mind," Orange said. "Her mother was of little use because of her depression and mental illness. Velma was the oldest girl so she took on the duties of mom at an age where she should have been playing with dolls."

ANGER, ABUSE, AND CHURCH

Despite her father's verbal abuse and alcohol-fueled beatings, the family kept up a face of religious interest. Velma would be sent to Bible school every year until the age of thirteen. During her last year of Bible school, her father marked the occasion by buying Velma a silk pink dress with ribbons. Velma recalled the day as one of the happiest of her life.

The happiness would be short-lived.

Velma would claim that her father raped her when she was thirteen years old. She revealed this only to her pastor in her later years before she stood trial. Velma did not even tell her mother whom she did not think would believe the molestation took place.

"Things that went on inside our home when I grew up," Velma said. "Were kept inside."

At the age of fifteen, Velma continued to excel in school. Despite her chubby physique, she becomes adept at basketball and is pegged to be the team's star player for the upcoming season. But her father did not allow her to play.

"Who is going to iron these damn clothes?" he snarled.

The family then moved to Robeson county and switched from the Presbyterian denomination to Baptist. It was here that Velma would meet Thomas Burke and the two made it clear that they wanted to date. Once again, Velma's father would intervene, telling Velma that she had to wait until her sixteenth birthday until she could date.

The two waited patiently for her birthday to arrive and the following year Thomas would propose to her while they went to the movies.

Knowing that her father would not approve, Velma and Thomas eloped, moving to Dillon, South Carolina. Neither Thomas or Velma had any money as they both quit high school to get married. Thomas then went to work at a local textile mill.

"At this point, I believe that Velma began to realize that her life would not be that much better with Thomas," Orange said. "He literally has the same job as her father."

Economics forced Velma and Thomas to move in with his parents. This arrangement would last for a year until Thomas got a better paying job at a soft drink company.

At the age of nineteen, Velma would give birth to her first son, Ronnie. The couple would then move back to Parkton, North Carolina where they would remain in the same home for eleven years. Two years later, the young couple would welcome a daughter named Kim.

A CYCLE OF RELIGION AND ABUSE

The Burkes would be fixtures at the local Baptist church with Velma taking the reigns to teach a Sunday school class. But the prayers and sermons would do little to offset the growing ennui in the Burke home. Two years after giving birth to Kim, Velma would get hit by a drunk driver while crossing the street. She would be hospitalized for an extended period, suffering both physically and mentally.

Thomas' job at the soft drink company would not be enough to provide for the family. Velma would be forced to leave her small children at home and work in a textile mill just like her father. The couple would have different work hours, with Velma working nights and Thomas working days as they would take turns watching the children.

Velma would fall victim to the hard work at the mill and the stress of raising two young children. She began bleeding and her doctor performed a hysterectomy.

Velma's mother would take pity on the couple and give them one acre of land near their old farm. Thomas would build a three-bedroom home for the family but Velma was already going down a slippery slope. Her personality changed after the hysterectomy, claiming that she always felt "nervous and afraid."

Things would get worse as Thomas suffered a head injury in a car accident. He then began to drink heavily and begin to beat Velma.

"It was deja vu," Orange said. "Velma had, in essence, married her father."

One night, the couple argued and Thomas punched Velma in an alcohol-fueled tantrum. The police are called to the home and Velma sent Thomas to the state hospital to get treatment for his drinking. Her husband remains there for three days but when he returns home, his behavior is worse than behavior. He's angry at Velma for sending him to the "drunk tank". His alcoholism worsens and he would go on to lose his job because of absenteeism.

"Velma is thirty-five years old at this time," Orange said. "But she's an old thirty-five with crow's feet under her eyes and a hangdog look. She's had a rough life, not necessarily by her own design, and it has taken its toll."

Velma leaves the textile mill but then finds two different jobs in order to support the family. During the day, she works as a sales clerk in a Belk department store. At night, she goes to work as a machine operator in a cotton mill.

Thomas, meanwhile, would continue to drink.

He rages on a daily basis, on one occasion he pinned son Ronnie up against the wall and threatened him with a knife. Velma would faint during the encounter and be transported to the hospital. She was diagnosed as having a nervous breakdown and lapsed into a serious depression. The medical staff gave her tranquilizers to calm down. Velma believed that it was during this stint in the hospital that she became addicted to the painkillers.

"The drugs were helping," Orange said. "When nothing else did. So she wanted more and more."

Velma's children acknowledged that their mother's mood swings were due to the drugs.

Over the next three years, Velma would go in and out of the hospital for drug overdoses. After each visit, her addiction only grew as did her prescription list.

"She fell through the cracks in her own family," Orange said. "And in the system itself. Her family had their own issues to deal with as Thomas would abuse everyone on a daily basis. Finally, Velma did something she could control. She killed her husband."

On April 21st, 1969, Velma would drop a cigarette on the floor of her home and waited until her husband inhaled enough smoke to die.

His death, however, would do nothing to solve Velma's problems.

Her addictions and anxiety would only get worse.

A HOSPITAL FREQUENT FLYER

Velma would have another nervous breakdown after killing Thomas and lapse into a guilt-ridden depression. But seven months later, a co-worker at the Belk department store would introduce her to fifty-four-year-old Jennings Barfield. Jennings had emphysema and diabetes but Velma would marry him anyway. Unlike her marriage with Thomas which started out well, Velma's marriage with the older Jennings would be troubled from the start. Her drug addiction would escalate and Jennings would express his own regret at marrying her.

"I don't know why I married her," Jennings said. "All she does is pop pills all day."

After less than three years of marriage, Velma decided to part ways with Jennings. She didn't file for divorce, however, she decided to poison him with arsenic. She would later claim that she only meant to "make him sick."

Jennings Barfield was already ill and doctors had no suspicion that Velma was behind the death. Arsenic was a slow burn poison that could kill without detection. The autopsy called for no arsenic test and Velma had gotten away with murder once again.

But Seven months later, Velma would overdose on her prescription meds and become hospitalized. Her family recognized the pattern but could not wean Velma off of the drinks. She would remain hospitalized for three weeks.

Her personality seemed to change after the hospital release. She returned to work at Belk department store but kept being combative and argumentative with customers. Her boss knew of her circumstances and tried to coax her to do better. He took her away from the public contact and into the back stock room where he had her put pricing on the clothing items.

Her boss soon realized that Velma's addiction had gotten out of control. Velma would not be able to function in the back room, leaving tasks uncompleted as she would have her prescription medications delivered to the store.

"It is a hopeless situation," the store manager told Velma's son Ronnie before he fired his mother.

BROKE AND DESTITUTE

With no income, Velma would lose the family home as she no longer paid the mortgage. She would be forced to move back in with her parents and face the two people she blamed everything for.

Her father had grown ill, however, and would die from lung cancer shortly after Velma moved back into the home. She would feel bad about her father's death and admit that she had a love/hate relationship with him.

"I had learned to love him as much as I had hated him," Velma said. "He was so good to my kids. I think he tried to do with my kids like he wished he had done to us. He could not stand to see me correct them. If I would pick them up and spank them, he would ask me, 'Isn't that enough?'"

But after her father's death Velma self-medicated once again. She overdosed and was hospitalized for two weeks. Her family didn't judge, they instead thought she was "cursed."

"Velma needed psychiatric help," Orange said. "So she began medicating herself with deleterious results. She would "doctor shop" for different physicians who would be manipulated into giving her the drugs she wanted. Her addiction eventually grows until she becomes desperate for money in order to fuel the drug habit."

A MURDERER AND A THIEF

Velma began stealing from those closest to her, starting with her mother. Her mother confronted Velma about a missing check and Velma went ballistic.

"She had violent mood swings," Orange said. "The medication had completely changed her personality as she needed the drugs above all else. The people around her were not familiar with how to handle a person who had this kind of mental illness. So this made for a very dangerous cocktail for her and anyone close to her."

Hitting a new low, Velma took out a $1,000 loan under her mother Lillie's name. She put up the family home as collateral and forged her mother's signature on the documents. Velma then blew through the money and a month later took out another loan, once again using her mother's house as collateral. The following month, she emptied the checking account on her now deceased husband, Jennings. Two months later, the loan company began sending Velma overdue notices as she had not been paying off the loan.

"In Velma's mind," Orange said. "She had no other choice but to kill off her own mother."

Velma went to the local pharmacy and looked for bottles that had the warning of "fatal if ingested." She put the poison into a drink for her mother and watched as she drank the fatal elixir.

Her mother then began vomiting and lost control of her bowels. Within a few hours, her mother could not so much as walk and an ambulance was called.

Velma came to visit her in the hospital to finish the job. Armed with a Thermos, she made a special concoction of chicken soup and arsenic.

"Drink it slow," Velma said as she tenderly lifted the cups to the lips of her ailing mother. "Slow."

Her mother would eventually die of "natural causes" as no one suspected Velma of committing murder. Instead, she received sympathy.

"So sorry for your loss," hospital staff said.

"The thing with arsenic is that it shuts down the whole system," Orange said. "So hospital staff just chalked up her mother's weakness to old age. Checking for arsenic poisoning would be the furthest thing from their mind."

Velma showed the necessary emotion and received sympathy from friends and family. She then moved in with her daughter Kim and son-in-law Dennis who lived in a trailer park. She could not evade the authorities for long though as the authorities caught wind of Velma's check forgeries.

Velma reacted as she always did. She would run away and medicate herself.

"Her drug addiction kept pushing her into a corner and she saw no way out," Orange said. "So, this time, she goes to her son Ronnie's house and overdoses again, trying to kill herself. She falls and breaks her collar bone which laid her out in the hospital another three weeks."

But the police find her situation unsympathetic.

"We're sorry, Velma," the deputy informed her at her hospital bed. "But once you have been cleared for release, we will arrest you."

Velma would not have that. She tried to overdose again but this go around the hospital staff pumped out her stomach.

She was sent to court the next day and sentenced to six months in jail for the forgery. She is released after four months for good behavior.

NO REHAB HERE

Her addiction still unchecked, Velma returned to live with Kim and her son-in-law. She rummaged through the belongings of her son-in-law and stole a check, forging his name so she can get more prescription meds. Her daughter Kim now has caught wind of her mother's addiction, pleading with her doctors to stop prescribing her.

"In some ways," Orange said. "The doctors were just as guilty as she was. But back in the day, there was no way to cross-reference this stuff like we do now. Once she had her fill with one doctor she would go to the next and the next."

Velma's addiction prevented her from taking a forty-hour a week job. So she looked for alternative forms of income.

She would find a job taking care of the elderly.

Montgomery and Dolly Edwards would be her first clients.

"She found herself some easy targets," Orange said. "There didn't seem to be any legislative body in place that prevents sociopaths from caretaking the elderly. So Velma doesn't slip through any cracks, she just befriends the elderly couple and begins taking care of them."

Montgomery was blind and unable to walk. He was 93-years old and his 83-year old wife was too feeble to take care of him. They paid $75 a week for Velma to become their live-in caretaker.

All was good, at least in the beginning. But Dolly had a sharp tongue and would criticize Velma daily. Velma would keep a nice exterior unless confronted, saw Dolly has yet another wheel in her cycle of verbal abuse.

"It seemed to be a never-ending loop for her," Orange said. "Being forced to deal with verbally abusive people. Velma had long since snapped and Dollie simply had no idea who she was dealing with."

Velma began to plot out Montgomery and Dollie's demise until she meets their nephew, Stuart Taylor.

Stuart was already married but was blown away when he met the caretaker of his Aunt Dollie.

Velma would play it cool, stealing what she could from the couple in terms of petty cash and household items that had value. They outlived their usefulness to her within a year as Montgomery died of "natural causes". One month later, Dolly also passed away.

And again, no one suspected the sweet and soft-spoken Velma to have had anything to do with their deaths.

MOVING ON

Velma saw being a caretaker as a perfect front for her. She could steal as much money as she could and when the old folks detected something amiss she would simply poison them. After killing the Edwards' couple, she set the word out at church that she as available to be a caregiver. The pastor would refer her to Margie Lee Pittman who was seeking for a caregiver for her elderly parents, John Henry and Record Lee.

"She comes here twice a week," the pastor reassured Pittman. "She's a nice, kindly woman. You can't go wrong."

Pittman's father, John Henry Lee, was eighty years old when he discovered that his new caregiver had forged a $50 check on his account. He then fell violently ill, suffering through a spastic spell of vomiting, diarrhea, and convulsions. The doctors would chalk up his quick death to gastroenteritis but in fact, he had been poisoned with arsenic.

Velma played the caregiver role until his end. She attended his funeral and cried with the family, sending an ornate wreath (with money stolen from the dead man) to the proceedings.

For whatever reason, Velma spared Lee's wife and moved back to Lumberton, North Carolina to live in a trailer park. She began working as an aide in a nursing home and received word from Stuart that he was now a widow. The two began dating and she moved part of her belongings into his home.

"Stuart is a nice guy," Orange said. "He has no idea what kind of woman Velma is. She is so manipulative and cunning that the younger man is putty in her hands. So the relationship starts great as she reels him in with kindness and charm."

The couple are happy cohabitating until Stuart Stuart finds a letter addressed to Velma from the state penitentiary.

Curious, he began reading the correspondence and realized that is from a former cellmate of Velma.

Stuart became enraged. He threatened to "expose" Velma to all of his family and friends. Somehow, someway, however, she was able to calm him down.

He then found out that she had forged over $200 in checks on his account. The two argued but stayed together for the next two months.

"Velma had the Christian facade down pat," Orange said. "She asked Stuart to forgive her and the next thing you know they are going to a Rex Humbard revival. But before they went, she poured arsenic poison in both his beer and tea. She made sure he drank every drop."

Returning home from the revival, Stuart started to vomit on the drive home, the poison kicking in.

Velma had to keep the con going. She had to appear like a concerned girlfriend so she called up Stuart's daughter, Alice, later that night and told her that Stuart had came down with the flu.

Stuart's daughter expressed concern but Velma kept her at bay.

"Don't you worry now, honey. I'll take care of everything."

Stuart died the next day.

Velma would speak at Stuart's funeral and tearfully asked for his wedding band. His family graciously allowed her to have it and gave her $400 to help her cope with the grief.

But Alice knew her father was a picture of health. She vociferously argued for more tests beyond the standard autopsy and sure enough, arsenic had been found in Stuart's tissues.

On March 10th, 1978, the sheriffs arrived at Velma's home to bring her in for questioning. She was interrogated for over three hours, holding her ground. But she knows the evidence will trump her denials and tries to commit suicide after being released. This go around, however, her son Ronnie stopped her.

The sheriffs come to visit Velma again and she has one more surprise up her sleeve.

But Velma has one more surprise up her sleeve.

She would confess. Not only for the murder of Stuart but of six others.

"I set my first husband on fire," Velma confessed without an attorney present. "And I killed the rest of them."

"It was almost as if she wanted to be free of the guilt she had been carrying," Orange said. "Her confession seemed to take a burden off her back."

"The last ten years were like that," Velma said. "A drug nightmare. It was a case of not knowing where you are or what you've done."

The bodies of her victims were later exhumed and all tested positive for arsenic.

FACING THE GRIM REAPER

Velma's case would be prosecuted by Joe Freeman Britt, who was listed in the Guinness Book of World Records as the country's "deadliest prosecutor."

Velma would plead not guilty by reason of insanity but the court denied her plea.

"I needed to keep them sick until I could pay back the money I had stolen from them," Velma said. "I wanted to earn their thanks by nursing them back to health. I needed the money. I was addicted to pain killers. Anti-depressants. Amphetamines."

On November 23rd, 1978, Velma's trial would begin in Elizabethtown, North Carolina where she would be charged with the first-degree murder of her boyfriend, Stuart Taylor. The trial lasted seven days and the jury reached a verdict of guilty, placing her on death row at the age of 47. She was scheduled to be executed on February 3rd, 1979 but received a stay.

Velma would be sentenced to death and the verdict was appealed all the way to the U.S. Supreme court. Her attorney maintained that the jury had never been presented with the full extent of Velma's "addiction and background." Velma remained tight-lipped about that to everyone but her pastor. Her attorney felt thought her horrific background could have been used as part of her defense and the jury would have found her to be more of a sympathetic case.

CHANGING SPOTS?

"She's not the same person who went to prison in 1978," Kim Burke Norton, Velma's daughter said.

While in jail, Velma became a model prisoner.

"The first week I was here was the worst week," Velma recalled. "Everything about it."

Velma no longer had access to her drugs in prison and she began to dry out. With daily visits from two different pastors, Velma began to discuss her anger and repressed issues that fueled her addiction and murders.

Velma would claim that as she was awaiting trial in 1978 she came to a "meeting with Christ" that caused her to "change inwardly."

Velma heard a broadcast by radio evangelist JK Kinkle. "Jesus loves you, prisoners, too," Kinkle said. "He died for you too. No matter what you've done, the Lord will forgive you."

After Velma heard this sermon, she dropped to her knees and cried out to God.

She would then become the "go to" counselor for young inmates in the prison.

The inmates would nickname Velma as "Mama Margie" because of her wisdom and she would in turn think of them as her "adopted children."

The prison guards and counselors would take the most incorrigible prisoners and place them in a cell next to Velma. Velma would invariably counsel the young prisoner and advise them on the correct path.

"They'd come in ready to kill themselves," Sister Mary Teresa Floyd said. "And here she was with a death sentence, mothering and helping them."

"Living in prison is a struggle," Velma said. "Even at its best. And I know that without Him and His strength that has sustained me, I couldn't have made it even this far."

Her stay on death row soon became a part of the news brief. During this time, a phalanx of evangelists would take her cause to the mainstream. The Reverend Hugh Hoyle would become Velma's personal minister as she received stays of execution in September, October and December of 1981. She would also have a letter correspondence with Ruth Graham, Billy Graham's wife as well as meeting their daughter Ann.

While Velma impressed the Christian do-gooders, the family members of the victims were not taken in by her "conversion."

"She's got religion now, they say," Margie Lee Pittman said. "Well, she had religion before. So we all thought."

A few more stays were granted until 1984 when the U.S. Supreme Court justice Warren Burger granted her a stay until August of that year. At this point, however, her execution seemed inevitable. In an ironic move, Velma would choose poison rather than the gas chamber and enjoyed the final visits from her children and grandchildren.

During the final week before her execution, the Reverend Hoyle, and his wife came to the prison with a battery-powered portable keyboard. His wife played the little organ then the Reverend sang "He Hideth My Soul" and "He is So precious to Me" in the cramped visitor booth.

Velma sang along, whistling in the graveyard before the reaper came for her.

She then wrote letters to each of the victim's family asking them for forgiveness. Reverend Hoyle would deliver the letters to the families, all of whom would refuse them.

MEET THE HANGMAN

As her execution date neared, Velma was placed in a solitary cell that stood directly across from the death chamber.

"It's total isolation," Velma said. "From everyone I had been with for six years."

North Carolina Governor James B. Hunt would reject her final plea for clemency.

On the day of her execution, the jail house would turn into a media frenzy. Death penalty advocates gathered outside the prison and chanted "Hip, hip, hurrah...K-I-L-L" while some sloganeered with "burn, bitch, burn". The protesters held up a few placards that quote

Romans ch.13 which ironically was a verse that Velma would repeat to guards during her prison stay.

"For rulers are not a terror to good works, but to the evil…(The ruler) beareth no the sword in vain, for he is the minister of God, a revenger to execute wrath upon him that doeth evil."

The execution was scheduled to take place at 2:00 a.m but the protesters remained outside, their chants reduced to a simple "Kill her! Kill her!"

On November 2nd, 1984, Velma would be executed by lethal injection. The prison official came out and addressed the press, giving out copies of Barfield's statement of apology. The reporters then eagerly anticipated what Velma requested for her last meal. Initially, Velma just wanted the normally scheduled prison food; chicken livers, collard greens and a sheet cake with peanut butter icing. The last meal was delivered but Velma immediately lost her appetite. Instead, she opted for Cheese Doodles and a glass of Coca-Cola.

"Her attorney believed that Velma could have done some good in life," Orange said. "He stated that she could have become a teacher, counselor or a pastor. But her father set her on a path of self-destruction that she couldn't escape from. By the time she the left that road to ruin, she was too far gone in terms of her murderous acts. Justice had to be served in the end. In the end, the law doesn't care how genuine you are in your pleas for forgiveness. It only cares about the rule of law."

"I'm sorry for the hurt that I've caused," Velma said before her execution. "So many people, today if it were possible, I wish I could take every bit of hurt on myself."

FOREVER MISSING: THE DISAPPEARANCE OF NATALEE HOLLOWAY

NATHAN NIXON

Natalee Holloway Disappearance

The tragic story of Natalee Holloway still remains a mystery to this day. The events prior to her disappearance are centered on unreliable witnesses, investigators not following proper procedures, and friends who had left her alone with local patrons. To say that a school trip is never supposed to turn out this way is a monumental understatement. Several theories exist as to what really happened to Natalee. The one, glaring truth of the matter is that Natalee was a beautiful, vibrant young woman who is gone far too soon. Many other facts exist. Witnesses, however, do not.

Natalee Holloway was born in 1986 to David and Elizabeth Holloway in Clinton, Mississippi. Following her parents mutual divorce in 1993, she was raised by her mother alongside her younger brother. Natalee made her life in Alabama when her mother re-married to George Twitty. It was here that she prospered in many organizations, extracurricular activities, and academic niches. Natalee attended Mountain Brook High School in Mountain Brook, Alabama. She was a prominent member in the National Honor Society, was a leader on the school dance team, and competed several sports. Through her hard work, she had earned a full scholarship to attend the University of Alabama, where she enter a pre-med course track and eventually earn her Doctorate. This was all assuming she would make it to the next fall.

Upon graduation, 124 graduating Mountain Brook High School seniors took an "unofficial" school trip to Aruba. Aruba is a Dutch holding in the Caribbean. The group of students arrived in Aruba on May 26, 2005. The trip was scheduled for five days. Oddities of this trip were already apparent. While the trip had 7 chaperones, the students were not expected to be watched every second. The chaperones would meet with the full group of students each night to make sure that everything was okay. To say that these students were taking advantage of this was an understatement. "There was wild partying, lots of drinking, lots of room switching every night," Police Commissioner

Gerold Dompig, who headed the investigation from mid-2005 to late 2016, said. "We are aware that the Holiday Inn told them they were absolutely not welcome back next year. Natalee, we know, drank all day every day while there. We have statements that proclaim she started every morning with cocktails. Often times so much drinking that she didn't show up for breakfast on two separate mornings."

Liz Cain and Claire Foreman, two of Holloway's classmates, agreed. "The drinking was excessive. We all were going too far and didn't understand the dangers"

Jodi Bearman organized the class trip. The investigation that would soon follow turned up numerous mistakes and irresponsibility's on the part of organizers and chaperones. The obvious problem was the supervision. How can seven chaperones have control of 124 high school graduates in a foreign place? These students were essentially given the freedom to do whatever they wanted with no punishment. Investigators and parents alike could not believe the lack of supervision and authority displayed by the adults. The punishment that Natalee Holloway would suffer was far greater than anyone could have imagined. However, the fact that this was an avoidable mistake is obvious. Natalee Holloway should never have been allowed to be in this position.

It was May 29, 2005. Natalee had packed her luggage and prepared all of her things to board the flight home the next morning. She had positioned her luggage neatly at the foot of her bed and cleaned up her hotel room accordingly. The 124 graduates had one last night of fun before it was time to head home. This was the last time she would be in her hotel room.

Natalee went out on the town with several of her classmates on night of May 29. Typical of the previous nights, she and her classmates had been heavily drinking and interacting with numerous locals. Natalee had a contagious personality and could always strike up a conversation with anyone. As the night drew on into morning, they arrived at Carlos'n Charlies. This was a well-known bar and dance club in the heart of Aruba. Natalee would last be seen at approximately 1:30 A.M. on May 30, 2005. The story was only just beginning.

Natalee had met up with locals seemingly every night she went out. Striking up conversations, drinking excessively, and trusting strangers was common by several of the graduates that were there. The last glimpse of Natalee would prove to be the beginning of a complicated, international investigation that would prove nearly impossible to solve. She left the club that morning with 17-year-old Joran van der Sloot, 21-year-old Deepak Kalpoe, and 18-year-old Satish Kalpoe. The events that took place after that are largely contested. Through many different testimonies by witnesses and suspects, investigators would check every lead and run into heartbreaking dead ends.

Upon the morning sunrise, the graduates arrived to board the flight home. It was time to start the rest of their lives. All of the graduates arrived without problem except for one: Natalee Holloway. Through irresponsible chaperoning of a class trip and complete disregard for holding the safety of these students paramount above a fun time, an 18-year-old girl was missing. Her hotel room looked untouched from the previous evening. Her luggage safely packed in anticipation of leaving. No signs of movement in the room. Not even a towel had been disturbed. It was frighteningly clear that she had not returned to her room from the previous night's adventures. When the students and chaperones realized what was going on, they immediately notified authorities. Aruban police initiated immediate searches of the island and its surrounding waters. No trace of her was found.

Joran van der Sloot is undoubtedly the most central figure to this case. Van der Sloot was a 17-year-old Dutch honors student who lived in Aruba. At first glance, his baby face and focused eyes would seemingly make him very approachable to anyone. This was, apparently, not the first night that Natalee and Joran had met. In previous nights, they hung out at bars and engaged in behavior not known to most high school students. Over the course of the next several years, Joran would lead investigators and the Holloway family on a wild goose chase that involved changing alibis, secret videos, and fraud. The innocent appearance that Joran van der Sloot displayed was only a disguise for the true monster he would prove to be.

The Kalpoe brothers were Surinamese friends of van der Sloot. Their significance is much less publicized beyond the last sighting of Holloway. Natalee was last seen getting into Deepak Kalpoe's car with both van der Sloot and Satish. This has been confirmed true by both witnesses and suspects in one way or another. There are numerous stories told by van Sloot and other later suspects that bring the Kalpoe's back to the forefront of the case. In such a complicated investigation, Joran van der Sloot, Deepak Kalpoe, and Satish Kalpoe emerged as early suspects.

Action was fast when news reached family of the mysterious disappearance of Natalee. Her mother, Beth Twitty, immediately boarded a private jet with friends and departed for Aruba. Upon arriving in Aruba, the Twittys had started searching for themselves. They located the Holiday Inn and began asking questions. They had obtained footage from the nightclub she was last seen at. To Beth Twittys surprise, the Holiday Inn workers recognized Joran van der Sloot instantly. He had apparently been a regular in the area. The helpful Holiday Inn employees provided Beth and company with Joran's name and address. Within a mere four hours since arriving at Aruba, the Twittys had already obtained more information than investigators had been able to. The Twittys provided Aruba Police with this information. It appeared that a case was forming around Van der Sloot already. However, the mishandling of the case and poor techniques of the Aruba Police Department were already rearing their ugly head. This case would prove to be a showcase of poor work, bitter disappointment, and investigators being led around by the suspects themselves. The first lead, however, was officially created.

The Twittys and their friends went to the home of Joran van der Sloot. They were accompanied by two Aruban policemen. The fact that Van der Sloot was even allowed to be approached in this manner showed quickly the lack of thought given to the early stages of the investigation. At this early point in the case, the extent of the crime was largely unknown. Hoping for the best, the Twittys only wished to find Natalee safely at the home of Van der Sloot. Joran answered the door and initially denied even knowing who Natalee Holloway was. After being confronted with evidence of their rendezvous that morning, Van der Sloot admitted to being with Natalee. Also present at the house was Deepak Kalpoe, who was driving the vehicle that Natalee had entered in to.

Van der Sloot gave a sketchy story of what had happened after they left the nightclub. He informed the Twittys as well as the two policemen that they had taken Natalee to the California Lighthouse area. This area was near the nightclub, perhaps a few miles drive depending on the route taken. Natalee had been emphatic that she wanted to see sharks. After leaving the nightclub at 1:30 A.M. they went straight to this area to sight see. Van der Sloot informed them that they had returned Natalee to the Holiday Inn hotel where she had been staying at 2:00 A.M. Natalee, who was heavily intoxicated, stumbled exiting the vehicle. The men had offered to help Natalee to her room, however she refused their help and continued toward the entrance. It was at this time, according to Van der Sloot, that she was approached by a tall man wearing all black. Thinking this was a security guard, the men drove off. This, according to Van der Sloot, was the last interaction of any kind with Natalee Holloway that they had. Deepak Kalpoe affirmed the story and agreed with the events.

This is the initial story of the events. The initial investigation is, perhaps, the most ridiculed part in this case. Not only were the men not detained for further extensive questioning, they were completely presumed to be telling the truth. This not only wasted valuable time in finding Natalee, it also allowed suspects to plan their next move. The fact that Van der Sloot and Kalpoe had initially denied even knowing who Natalee Holloway was should have been the first sign of a problem. The second, and more major sign of a problem would come in the investigation of the hotel surveillance footage. While this was obviously looked at during the investigation, this is largely an accepted procedure that is typically done prior to confronting a potential suspect.

The surveillance footage, or lack thereof, was arguably the single biggest setback with this case. The fact that Natalee was not seen in any hotel footage that fateful morning would lend investigators to believe that Van der Sloot and Kalpoe were lying. The hitch in this was that many statements from the case could not even prove that all cameras were functional at the time. The next problem was the fact that not every entrance had a surveillance. This would leave reasonable doubt that Natalee could have been dropped off near one of these entrances that was simply inaccessible to the surveillance footage.

Investigators finally felt as though they had caught the break in the case they needed when a blood stain was found in Deepak Kalpoe's car. Searching the car that was captured on surveillance as the same one that transported Natalee Holloway from the nightclub, police discovered what appeared to be a blood stain. After lab testing and further investigation, not only was this not Natalee Holloway's blood, it could not even be proven to be blood at all. Another door was closed in the initial investigation of Natalee's disappearance.

After the first full day of investigation, United States involvement in the case began. Monetary assistance was given immediately to aid the Aruban Police Department. Additionally, American searchers sought to help with the advanced search of coastline that had been a constant since Natalee Holloway missed her flight. United States Secretary of State Condoleezza Rice stated "we are in constant contact with Aruban

Police. The safe return of Natalee Holloway continues to be our priority."

Hours after missing her flight, the media's involvement in the case was tremendous. All of the major news stations in the United States began their initial coverage of the story. With little facts to go on, it was largely reported as a missing person case with no evidence of foul play. No suspects had truly been pinpointed at this point. The news of her last being seen in the early hours leaving a nightclub led several to assume the worst from the get go, however. It would not be long before Joran van der Sloot was at the fore front of the investigation as well as the ensuing media storm.

It was just six days after Holloway's disappearance that authorities made their first arrest in the case. On June 5, 2005, Abraham Jones and Nick John were placed under arrest. To this day, the exact reasoning behind their arrest is unknown. One of the men had previous encounters with the law, while both were suspected of previously pacing hotels to pick up women. Both men were security guards at a nearby hotel, the Allegro Hotel. It is likely that the statements made by Van der Sloot and Kalpoe led police to this arrest. The men were released on June 13 with no charges being placed. This is yet another example of flawed work by the investigation. It was obvious that police were trusting of Joran van der Sloot and Deepak Kalpoe from the onset. This is a largely debated topic to this day. Many wonder why Van der Sloot and Kalpoe were not arrested initially. However, this was just scratching the surface of what was to come.

On June 9, Joran van der Sloot and both Kalpoe brothers were arrested on suspicion of the kidnapping and murder of Natalee Holloway. In hindsight, it is absolutely unfathomable that it took investigators 10 days to make these arrest. The only evidence they really had at this point was surveillance of Natalee last being seen with these men. Aruban police reported that these men were the "prime suspects from the get-go." While this may have been true to a point, police waited until June 6 to start extended surveillance of the men. Investigators knew they would need much more evidence than a video of Natalee entering a car with the men from the nightclub. Aruban Police instigated phone taps, video surveillance, tailing their vehicles, and monitoring of their e-mails. At this point, in order to continue to hold the three suspects in custody, they would need to provide increasingly substantial evidence at different check points of the investigation. With increasingly consistent pressure from Natalee Holloway's family, police decided to stop the surveillance activities prematurely and execute the arrest on the men.

The arrest of these three suspects was met with heavy interest from people all over the world. The procedures by police and the heavy involvement of the Holloway family seemingly left everyone with an opinion on what should have been conducted differently. Many media outlets focused on the timing of the surveillance activities. Having taken nearly a week to begin the activities from the time of Natalee's last sighting, many felt it was already too late to incriminate the suspects. Also, the fact that surveillance started at the time they had already arrested Adams and John was a bit odd for normal investigative procedure. Lastly, many assumed that if investigators pursued an arrest after just a few days of surveillance of the men, they must have captured something indisputable to implicate one or all of the suspects. This was simply not the case. Aruban Police had missed the initial window of the investigation. Many critics argue that in the interest of uncovering the truth, an extended surveillance would be necessary for the time period they had waited to begin. Investigators instead buckled to pressure from an unorthodox family interaction in a complicated case.

June 11 was the first of many highly publicized false leads. Aruban Minister of Justice David Cruz indicated, in a statement, that Natalee Holloway was dead and that authorities knew the exact location of her body. This was all over most any major media outlet as an early morning breaking news story. The United States was gripped with curiosity and heartbreak as it seemed the terrible truth had come to fruition. Hours later, Cruz released a follow up statement that they had been the victim of "misinformation." This simply is unacceptable. As an investigator or someone in a position as high as Cruz was, you can't put the wagon before the horse, especially to national media outlets. What was the source of this misinformation? Lead investigator Gerold Dompig reported to the Associated Press that one of the detained men had informed them that "something terrible and unthinkable" had happened on the beach after they left the nightclub. The suspect, it was reported, was leading them to the location of the body. This, of course, was another folly.

On June 16, yet another suspect, Steve Gregory Croes, was arrested. "Croes was detained based on urgent information given to us by one of the other three suspect," Aruban Police Superintendent Jan van der Straaten informed the media. While this arrest didn't yield much as far as new leads, it did start to give the appearance that investigators were at a standstill with the case. Six days later on June 22, Joran van der Sloot's father, Paulus, was arrested. This was largely believed to be a bargaining chip to use against Joran. While Paulus was not a suspect, as later revealed by police, he was interrogated in an effort to get more information on Joran. Both Croes and Paulus van der Sloot were released on June 26.

It was around this time where public opinion began to focus on Joran van der Sloot. It was quite clear to all involved that Van der Sloot was not being truthful in his story. The events made little sense to the general public. The longer that Natalee remained missing, the more likely it was that she was, indeed, dead. The suspicion on Joran would only intensify in the coming day.

From the time of the arrest of Joran van der Sloot and the Kalpoe brothers, their stories changed numerous times. In particular, Van der Sloot was giving three completely conflicting stories that would put the focus solely on him.

The first story shift came, oddly enough, from all three suspects. Van der Sloot and both Kalpoe brothers all agreed that Joran and Natalee had been dropped off at the Marriott Hotel beach near several fisherman huts. Van der Sloot was emphatic that he didn't harm Natalee Holloway in any way. He told investigators that they were both heavily intoxicated, and eventually Natalee passed out on the beach. When this happened, he began to walk home. It was at this time that he made a phone call to Deepak Kalpoe that he was walking home. Van der Sloot claims to have sent Kalpoe a text message 40 minutes later. Oddly enough, the phone call nor text message was found in Van der Sloot's phone records.

Lead investigator Gerold Dompig gave insight into the third different story by the suspects. This story, told by Joran van der Sloot, was a turning point in that it showed that he was willing to change his story however he saw fit in order to avoid suspicion.

"The latest story came when Joran saw that his buddies, the Kalpoe's, were essentially pointing the finger in his direction. He wanted to screw them by pointing the finger right back at them. But the story simply doesn't check out. He just wanted to screw Deepak. They (Deepak and Joran) had great arguments about this in front of the judge. Their stories didn't match. Joran felt the focus shifting to him and was willing to do anything to change it. That girl, she was from Alabama. She is not going to stay in the car with two black kids while Joran simply gets out of the car to head home alone. We firmly believe the second story; that they were dropped off at the Marriott. This goes along with the timeline and the stories given by the Kalpoe's."

Upon hearings in front of the judge on July 4, both Satish and Deepak Kalpoe were released from custody. Joran van der Sloot was to remain for a minimum of 60 days. Focus was solely on Van der Sloot as the main suspect in the disappearance of Natalee Holloway.

For nearly all of July, searches for Natalee Holloway remained fruitless endeavors. Investigators had no leads and were consistently getting varied stories from Joran van der Sloot. While police had solid suspicions of Van der Sloot, they had essentially zero solid evidence against him. The media storm updated the world daily on search efforts. With each passing day, reality began to set in for many that Natalee Holloway may never be found. Initially, a $50,000 reward was offered for Natalee's safe return. On July 25, the reward for the safe return of Holloway had increased all the way to $1,000,000. In addition, a $100,000 reward was offered for information that would lead to the location of her remains. In August of the same year, the reward for the location of her remains would raise all the way to $250,000. This was widely covered by the media and many local and national governments. This was a final attempt by investigators to break the cold case open. This strategy had several negative impacts, however. The most severe of these were the wasted time on false leads and folly calls. This was not anticipated by investigators as it should have been.

Between July 27 and 30, investigators initiated a massive undertaking. The pond in front of the Aruba Racquet Club was completely drained. This was within one mile of the Marriott Hotel where Van der Sloot had apparently taken Natalee Holloway. A tip was given to police that was especially unique. A gardener had apparently seen Joran van der Sloot driving into the Racquet Club with the Kalpoe brothers. Van der Sloot was said to have been hiding his face. The gardener informed police that the men were seen driving in between 2:30 A.M. and 3:00 A.M. on the morning of May 30. The search of the pond bed and surrounding area, however, yielded no clues.

On July 28, a jogger came forward with a frightening testimony. The United States media covered this story heavily for several days as it was the first story of someone seeing a woman resembling Natalee Holloway since her disappearance. The jogger claimed that she saw a group of men burying a young, blonde haired woman on the afternoon of May 30 at a landfill. The landfill was subsequently searched three separate times with precision. This search, again, yielded no results.

In late August, Joran van der Sloot became the front page villain to many. Throughout the entire case, it was well covered as to how many variations of a story Joran had given. While showing no remorse or empathy for the Holloway family, the public formed a very negative opinion of Van der Sloot. Anita van der Sloot would provide more material for the family. "It's a desperate attempt to get the boys to talk. But there is nothing to talk about. Joran has no fault in this mystery." Joran van der Sloot's mother made this statement after police again brought in the Kalpoe's for questioning. This left a bitter taste in the mouths of many. It was shaping up to be Van der Sloot's versus investigators.

On September 3, 2005, Joran van der Sloot was released from custody due to insufficient evidence to hold. By September 14, all restrictions were officially lifted from Van der Sloot. Whatever the events of May 30, no suspect was in custody and there were no leads for police. Joran van der Sloot was a free man. The release of Van der Sloot created a frenzy among the general public. People all over the United States and surrounding areas were furious, set in their beliefs that a guilty man was walking away free. The nation was gripped against a common villain.

The months that followed Joran van der Sloot's release provided media cannon fodder of epic proportions. Van der Sloot did several interviews and even composed a book of his take on the events of the night. To the public's astonishment, this man was now profiting off of this whole fire storm of a case. The most notable post release interview came with Fox News on a three night special. Van der Sloot claims that the two were heavily intoxicated on the beach after leaving the nightclub. He went into great detail about the two planning an escapade on the beach, narcotic use, and partying in a fun filled night in Aruba. He showed little empathy or remorse for any of the events. He seemingly talked about Natalee as if she was the villain. Joran went on to explain that Natalee wanted to have sex on the beach, however he didn't have a condom. He left her on the beach and was driven home by Satish Kalpoe. Later, Satish Kalpoe's lawyer claims that Satish was asleep well before this would have happened. Joran went on to explain that he was embarrassed for having left a beautiful woman alone on the beach, citing this as the reason for his ever changing story. He said that he was convinced Holloway would turn up.

This all sat so negatively to viewers. There was outrage over the handling of the investigation. People could not understand how no evidence existed to implicate a man that was deemed the perpetrator. Aruba authorities later claimed that over $3 million had been spent on the investigation. This was over 40% of the overall budget for investigative expenditures.

On December 18, 2007 after extensive efforts to implicate the Kalpoe brothers and/or Joran van der Sloot, the case was officially closed. Prosecutors cited lack of evidence to a violent crime, lack of evidence to a murder, as well as lack of continued funding for the expensive investigation. Over two full years after the disappearance of Natalee Holloway, the case was closed. The remains of Natalee Holloway had not been found. Joran van der Sloot not only was a free man, but had profited greatly from the publicity of the case. This, however, would not be the final chapter to the journey of Joran van der Sloot.

In the years after the closing of the Natalee Holloway case, Joran van der Sloot told several variations of events of that fateful morning. He gave countless interviews, seemingly telling a different story in each one of them. Ultimately, Joran van der Sloot was seeking money and fame through his disgusting actions. In an interview with Fox News in 2008, he claimed to have sold Natalee Holloway in sexual slavery. He later retracted the statements in the days after. It was reported in 2010 that in a 2009 interview with RTL group, he claimed he disposed of the body in a marsh area in Aruba. This interview was never confirmed, nor denied by investigators or Van der Sloot.

Remarkably, Van der Sloot would show his greed had no limits. On March 29, 2010 Van der Sloot contacted Beth Twittys legal representative. He offered to give the location to Natalee Holloway's remains in exchange for $25,000. After contacting police, the transaction was made. $15,000 was wired to Van der Sloot's account, and the remaining $10,000 was given by a middle man. The receipt of the transaction was videotaped by police. The information provided by Van der Sloot was proven false, as the building that he claimed housed the remains was not yet built at the time of the disappearance. Van der Sloot would be indicted on June 30 of the same year. However, he was about to be indicted for a much more serious crime.

On May 30, 2010, exactly five years from the time of the disappearance of Natalee Holloway, Stephany Flores Ramirez was reported missing in Lima, Peru. Ironically, she was found dead just three days later in a hotel room registered to Joran van der Sloot. On June 7, 2010, Van der Sloot confessed to killing Ramirez after he lost his temper while she was using his laptop. Within the same interview, he said that he knew where Holloway's body was. Dealing with jurisdiction issues, Peruvian police could not further investigate the Holloway statement without Aruban authorities.

Aruban authorities were granted interrogation of Van der Sloot in Peru in June of 2010. While he would not confess to murdering Holloway or her whereabouts, he did admit to the extortion plot on the Holloway family. "I wanted to get back at Natalee's family. They have been making my life miserable for the last five years," Van der Sloot said. Van der Sloot was found guilty in the murder of Stephany Flores Ramirez and sentenced to 28 years in prison. This sentence also included his time for his extortion of the Holloway family.

Natalee Holloway's remains have never been found. There have never been any convictions made into the disappearance of Natalee or any criminal wrong doing. In this case, it would be naïve to imagine a scenario where Joran van der Sloot was not responsible in some way for the death of Natalee Holloway. While Van der Sloot waste the best years of his life behind bars, a young woman with an extremely bright future is still gone. Closure will never be possible for the Holloway family. Perhaps a poor investigative strategy is to blame for the lack of any convictions. Maybe it is the irresponsible planning of school personnel and behavior supervision by chaperones could have prevented this tragedy. Better decision by Natalee herself may have helped avoid such a terrible event. In any case, an intelligent young woman who had everything in front of her did not deserve this end. The Holloway family did not deserve this. We will likely never know the true events of that fateful May morning. What we do know is that we will never get to see the true potential that Natalee Holloway had.

TARA GRINSTEAD

"I'm an 11th-grade history teacher at Irwin County High school. I also have a cheerleading squad of Junior Varsity cheerleaders. I just completed my first year of teaching, and I love every bit of it." - Tara Grinstead in a 1999 interview.

Tara Grinstead was a beauty pageant winner and high school teacher who strangely disappeared on October 22nd, 2005.

The mystery of her disappearance is as baffling now as it was over ten years ago. Tara was a beautiful woman in a small town and drew the attention of many men. But as investigators peeled back the onion on her life, they discovered that she had a complex personal life, one with many lovers and layers of relationship any one of whom may have sought to do her harm out of jealousy.

Investigators have pieced together the timeline of her activities prior to her disappearance. But the missing piece lies sometime during the night of October 22nd, 2005, when someone abducted Tara Grinstead and she would never be seen again.

What happened to Tara Grinstead?

EARLY LIFE

Tara was born on November 14th, 1974 to Faye and Billy Grinstead. She grew up in Hawkinsville, Georgia and was a popular cheerleader in high school as well as a diligent student. Her parents would divorce and her father would remarry a woman named Connie to whom Tara grew close to as well.

Tara loved animals, singing and going to church as a kid.

One cannot look upon pictures and video of Tara and not remark that she had a striking beauty. Graced with a voluptuous figure and long black hair, she had the ability to light up any room she walked into. She would eventually compete in beauty pageants, falling in love with the preparation, competition, and glamor of the activity.

"She had been into so many (pageants) that I had lost count," Connie Grinstead said.

Tara meticulously prepared for the pageants, remaining physically fit, taking speech lessons and learning how to sing. She would also graduate from Middle Georgia College and become a teacher at Irwin County High School in Ocilla. She would teach history to 11th graders but not give up on her pageant hopes.

In 1999, she would achieve the first step in her dream to enter the Miss USA contest, when she would win the local title of Miss Tifton.

This victory would allow her to compete in the Miss Georgia pageant. She would also receive scholarship winnings that she would use to help pay for her continuing college education.

"It was, for her, more than a dream come true," Tara's best friend Maria Hulett said. "It was the chance for her to be really proud of herself."

Footage of Tara during the Georgia pageant showed her to be an exuberant woman with a zest for life. She loved to exercise, drink Diet Coke with grenadine, collect Barbies and listening to 80s music like Bon Jovi. She had an infectious smile and played to the camera as she showed off her yellow business suit that she would wear for the pageant interview.

"Why did you pick yellow?" the reporter asked.

"Because it shows that I'm a happy person," Tara said.

With her pageant days behind her, Tara would earn a master's degree in education from Valdosta State University.

"She wanted to be a principal," her friend Oshja Anderson said. "She was well on her way."

Always seeking to improve herself, Tara would teach classes during the day and go to graduate school at night. She also held down a part-time job selling cosmetics at the local department store. By 2005, she had applied for a doctoral program in history and would occasionally fill in as the assistant principal.

"On the surface," forensic psychiatrist Orange said. "Tara's life looked to be a stellar one. She had a bright future in academia and during her pageant days, she learned to put forward the best appearance. But what lurked underneath in her personal life is the mystery."

MARCUS HARPER

At the heart of Tara's disappearance is figuring out the type of relationships she had with the numerous men in her life. She worked as a teacher, went to night school and worked the cosmetics counter at a department store. Outgoing and bubbly, she didn't have the personality type to reject anyone out of hand. She attracted men and had many suitors.

She did have a longtime boyfriend in Marcus Harper.

Harper was an Ocilla police officer who would later become an Army Ranger. Both of Tara's parents liked him as they both expressed the fact that he always remained respectful of them. They have consistently maintained that they never witnessed Harper treating Tara with disrespect.

Tara, however, had expressed to her sister that she was afraid of Marcus.

"She said she was afraid of him," Tara's sister Anita said. "What he had gone through with the Ranger training. He was capable of anything."

"Marcus was a strong Alpha-male type," Orange said. "A cop and an Army Ranger. Tara was rumored to have dated another cop as well but she didn't appear to have a type. From what we can gather, she dated a slew of men from older to younger, and from different walks of life."

About a year prior to her disappearance, Tara had broken up with Marcus. She had given him an ultimatum and wanted to be married. He did not want marriage but wanted to remain committed. The relationship would turn sour at that point.

Tara would begin to date other people. She was in a car with a romantic suitor named Rhett Roberts who was the son of her landlord. Marcus spotted the couple and would go ballistic, shouting obscenities at Tara.

Despite this angry confrontation, Tara would maintain ties with Marcus. In late July or early August of 2005 they would go to St. Augustine on a beach trip. After their date, Tara would confide to a friend that she was concerned about Marcus's temper.

Marcus would then be deployed back to Iraq a few weeks later. Tara would write the Army Ranger a letter in which she effectively ended their relationship.

According to Marcus, however, their relationship didn't come to a close until October of 2005. He had returned from the Middle East and called Tara to tell her that their relationship was over. Tara was at work and became so distraught that had to pull over to the side of the road. She called a friend who came and took her home. The next day, Tara would call off sick from her teaching job in order to "take a mental health day."

There was a rumor that a cop from a neighboring town, Heath Dykes, came to visit Tara at her school shortly afterward.

"These behaviors certainly show some mental fragilities on the parts of both Tara and Marcus," Orange said. "From what we can gather, it looked like an off-and-on style relationship with a few other romantic partners thrown in for good measure. It is unclear as to who was chasing who at various points of their relationship. If we are to believe Marcus, then she was chasing him. If we are to believe Tara's sister, then she was afraid of him. Why would you chase a man that you were afraid of? Something is not right here."

A few days later, Tara and Marcus would have another "heated argument" which she would tell one of her friends at her night class as well as another friend the next day while she had lunch.

According to Marcus, the argument centered around him breaking up with her. But Tara's sister Anita Gattis had a different story.

"They had a very bad argument," Anita said. "Several days before she went missing, concerning an 18-year-old that he was dating. My sister did not think that (the 18-year-old's) parents would approve of a 30-year-old dating an-18-year-old. I'm told that she threatened to tell the parents and they had a very heated argument over this."

Marcus said the argument was about something else entirely. He stated that she begged him not to end their relationship.

"She wanted me back and all," Marcus said. "And I said, 'I've started shopping outside of Ocilla, I think you need to do the same. Everybody in this town is connected to us one way or another."

"She approached me crying," Harper said as he repeated the same story on Greta Van Susteren's TV show. "She was very irrational, and she told me that if she found out I was dating someone, she would commit suicide."

But Tara's friend Osjha disputes the fact that Tara would do or say something like that.

"She's never said anything remotely similar to me ever any time."

Law enforcement authorities don't believe Tara committed suicide as she would have to go to extreme lengths to hide her own body and would have no motive to do so.

"There are a couple of contradictory things at play here," Orange said. "Tara was rumored to have dated some of her students so it would be hypocritical of her to criticize Marcus for dating someone in their teens. And it also doesn't make sense for her to come to Marcus' home begging to get back together. She had her share of suitors, some coming from out of town. She was a beautiful woman and she had options."

To her family's dismay, both the authorities and press would place Tara's life under a microscope. They had discovered that she had "several romantic relationships that occurred in relative proximity to one another."

"There was more rumors and innuendo," Orange said. "There were rumors that she was dating Rhett Roberts, her landlord's son. Rumors that she was dating one of her teenage students. Rumors that she was dating Heath Dyke, a police officer from another county. Even her own brother-in-law, Larry Gattis, was rumored to have an affair with Tara."

Both Larry and Tara's sisters are physicians. Larry specializes in geriatric medicine with only 3.3 out of 5-star reviews on Healthgrades. He was interrogated by investigators and expressed his outrage at the questions they were asking. One question was that if he had an affair with Tara and his response was judged by the polygraph as "deceptive."

ALL THAT AND A STALKER TOO...

Tara would have a stalker in a former student named Anthony Vickers. Friends recalled that Tara had taken special care to tutor Vickers but she later realized that the young man was "unstable."

"He was just kind of a troubled kid and that would be her nature," Osjha said.

Vickers was obsessed with his beauty queen teacher and claimed to have had a romantic relationship with her.

"She talked about the fact that he would call and he would rely on her and she knew it was getting too much for her," a friend named Maria said. "I just kept telling her, 'You know Tara, something's wrong.'"

Vickers was two years out of high school when he came to Tara's house and demanded to be let in. He pounded on the door until she called the police. Vickers resisted arrest but charges were later dropped and no restraining orders were ever filed.

The Vickers incident wasn't the only occasion that the former beauty pageant winner was being stalked. There was an incident where someone would call her home and make threats. The call was traced and it was determined to be a student in her homeroom who was promptly removed from the class.

THE NIGHT OF...

Before the night of her disappearance, Tara had enjoyed the company of her friend Dana and some teenage girls as they readied for the "Miss Georgia Sweet Potato" pageant. Her friend remembered Tara as being in a great mood, helping out the girls with their hair and makeup. She would attend the pageant where she served as a backstage coach. Later that evening, she went to the house of a neighbor before going to a barbecue a few blocks from her home. Police believe that she had remained at the barbecue until 11 pm when she left to go home. They would find the clothes she wore at the cookout on her bedroom floor which indicated to police that she had, in fact, returned home.

From that point on, police "have no idea" what happened to Tara.

On October 24th, 2005, Tara did not show up to teach her class. Her colleagues called the police who showed up at her residence to do a welfare check. They would find her white Mitsubishi parked in the garage, unlocked. Upon entering her home, police found a business card lodged in her door.

There appeared to be no sign of forced entry. Searching through the house, police found her cell phone plugged into her charger. Her purse and keys could not be found.

Strangely, the clothes she wore the night before were piled on the bedroom floor.

Investigators found it odd that the car door was unlocked and that the car seat was pushed back. Tara was petite at only five-foot-three and would have kept the seat much closer to the steering wheel. They found an envelope of cash (one hundred dollars) on her dashboard while both her dog and cat were inside. Tara's sister said that she was an animal lover who would never just abandon her pets.

Something was wrong...

The police immediately called the Georgia Bureau of Investigation as the lacked the resources to pursue this kind of crime.

Taking over the case, the GBI believed that Tara may have left with someone that she knew, given the lack of a forced entry and the fact that only her purse and keys were missing. Neighbors did not report hearing any screaming at night.

Her disappearance shocked the small and close-knit community. To a person, Tara was described as someone who had a great personality, loved by faculty and students alike. Nothing in her professional life would suggest that she had any enemies.

Volunteers from the community immediately went to work. Irwin County students, teachers, and other townsfolk searched the area and put out flyers.

"Missing. Tara Grinstead. $20,000 Reward."

ROUNDING UP THE SUSPECTS

Longtime boyfriend Marcus Harper was one of the first to be questioned. He came with a ready-made alibi for the night of Tara's disappearance.

Marcus was seen at a bar with friends then went on a 'ride-along' with a former partner on the local police force. His whereabouts was "essentially substantiated" according to authorities.

Former student/stalker Anthony Vickers was questioned but later ruled out as a suspect. Like the others, however, he could not account for the entire thirty-four hour period when Tara was last seen and reported missing.

"Vickers is probably the only one I would rule out," Orange said. "This disappearance was too clean. Vickers was a disturbed twenty-year-old man with a crush. He would not have the emotional wherewithal or the knowledge to pull off a crime with no clues. But someone with law enforcement or medical training could."

But who left the business card behind at her door?

The card was left by Heath Dykes, a married Perry police officer with two children. He was from the next town over and had known Tara since high school.

Neighbors would tell investigators that he visited Tara's house often. It is unclear what their relationship was (outside of the obvious innuendo and rumors).

Still, he had left close to two dozen messages on Tara's answering message on the weekend she went missing.

There is small-town gossip that the two were having an affair. Local witnesses have confirmed that they saw his wife throw his clothes out on the front lawn. The content of the messages he left have not been made public but the rumors were that he was telling her "he was sorry" and that he "loved her."

What is clear is that he did call Tara's mother from the front yard and ask if she knew where Tara was and if she was alright.

Heath Dykes was the last known person at Tara's home that night as he arrived a little after midnight.

"There are simply too many secrets here," Orange said. "Something was clearly going on in Heath's mind in order for him to call Tara that many times over the course of one evening. One rumor is that they were having an affair and that she was going to tell his wife. So he was calling her in a desperate attempt to stop her from doing that. Another possibility was that she was calling him for help and he was returning her calls. His involvement led to a lot of outlandish speculation, one of which was that Heath knew that a hit man was coming for Tara and that he was calling to make sure that she was okay."

"I think the fact that she was beautiful and other people paid attention to her would obviously make some people jealous," Tara's friend Maria said. "I think she was afraid of the possibility of someone hurting her from being angry at her, having reactions to her dating people."

Numerous men were rounded up and questioned, there was Jim Perry who dated Tara years earlier, Rhett Roberts, Marcus Harper, Anthony Vickers, and Eric Cook among others.

Another unsubstantiated rumor that Tara was involved with another student named Eric Cook. A friend of his had made mention of their affair in an Internet forum post where he stated that everyone knew that they were "messing around." He also said that the police didn't make the information public out of respect for Tara's family as she dated around quite a bit. An alleged friend of Cook disputed the rumor on the forum, however. Cook would later die in a car accident.

A neighbor, Joe Poirier lived with his wife and was rumored to have been "obsessed" with Tara. The older couple admitted to "looking out for Tara" and they were fond of her. He was seen pouring concrete near his home the day after she disappeared.

Another person of interest was Larry Gattis, the brother-in-law of Tara. He was brought in for questioning after the disappearance. It would later be revealed that he had been asked if he had an affair with Tara.

Larry answered 'no'.

The polygraph machine marked it as a 'deceptive answer.'

48 HOURS

In 2008, Tara's case would be featured on the CBS News show "48 Hours Mystery." The show would illustrate the parallels between Tara's case and the disappearance of Jennifer Kesse who would go missing in Orlando, Florida three months later. The GBI would also reveal during the broadcast that they had found a latex glove in Tara's yard just a few feet away from her front porch.

The GBI forensic team would analyze the DNA left in the glove and determine that it was a man's DNA, they just do not know who it belongs to. They would compare the DNA samples of the numerous men who were associated with or knew Tara but none of them have matched.

The DNA has also been entered into the Georgia and national databases but no match has been made to date.

"The glove may be a red herring," Orange said. "Whoever entered the home left nothing behind, no prints, DNA, nothing. So it was obviously someone who knew exactly what they were doing. They wanted to harm Tara."

A HOAX AND FALSE TIPS

In February of 2009, a man calling himself the "Catch Me Killer" began posting videos boasting that he had murdered sixteen women. One of the women he described had a close resemblance to Tara Grinstead. The man producing the video digitally obscured his face and voice but police eventually identified the culprit as twenty-seven-year-old Andrew Haley.

Haley performed the videos as part of a bizarre hoax and was eliminated as a possible suspect.

Investigator Gary Rothwell has expressed his lament at how the rumors and speculation have caused unfair stress to many who have been already tried in the public eye. "Irresponsible public accusations have been made about them, and they have no way to respond or defend themselves. And it's frustrating that we don't have evidence to rule anyone in or out."

Rothwell admits, however, that he has information that has not been released.

In February of 2015, authorities acted on a tip which led them to drain a pond in Fitzgerald, Georgia.

They didn't go into details as to what the specifics of the tip were. The pond would be drained and nothing would be found.

ALIBIS

Police have alibis from all the men who knew Tara Grinstead but no one has been ruled out because no one can account for the full thirty-four hour period.

Rhett Reynolds stated he went to sleep after the cookout. Joe Poirier was with his wife next door.

The most elaborate alibi, however, came from Marcus Harper.

Again, Marcus was in a local bar and a friend of Tara's had spotted him there. She would call Tara at around 10:15 and 10:30 to tell Tara that Marcus was there.

After 1 am, Marcus left the bar and went to look for his police officer friend, Sgt. Sean Fletcher. Fletcher was on duty that night.

Fletcher knew Tara as well. Ironically, he was one of the officers who arrived at Tara's house when Anthony Vickers, Tara's former student, was banging on her door.

There were rumors that Tara didn't like Fletcher because he had told Harper that Tara was entertaining Heath Dykes at her home.

Fletcher would deny that speculation.

"What we can extrapolate from this scenario was that Vickers was angry that his crush, Tara, was with another man," Orange said. "So he goes to her home and demands that she talk to him. He's young, twenty-years-old, and doesn't understand why she would do this to him. He is then arrested by Fletcher who relays what Tara is doing to Marcus, a man that Tara is wary about because of his temper. So now we have more than just a love triangle, it is a love octagon, with numerous men vying for and getting jealous over the attention of Tara."

At around 1:49 am, Fletcher received a call from dispatch informing him that Marcus Harper was looking for him. The two met up and walked Fletcher's beat, checking doors in downtown Ocilla.

Around 2:45, Fletcher was dispatch to a home where a mentally unbalanced man, Bennie Merritt, had stumbled into a home and refused to leave. Marcus would join Fletcher on the call as did two other officers. Merritt, however, was gone from the premises.

Minutes later, they began to search for Merritt who was also a neighbor of Tara's. The drunken Merritt would accost the cashier at the local gas station then be apprehended. Both Fletcher and Harper had responded to the call at the gas station and by the time they were done it was 4:28 am.

Marcus then headed home.

Investigators would later be able to corroborate these details with multiple witnesses, including Merritt, who was scrutinized as a possible suspect in the kidnapping as well.

Marcus Harper, however, has not been ruled out as a potential person of interest in the case.

"Marcus's alibi is too perfect," GBI investigator Maurice Godwin said.

Both Larry and Anita Gattis believe that Marcus is the top suspect.

"He had the motive," Tara's sister said. "And the training."

The insinuation would draw the ire of Marcus who became upset that Anita consistently brought up his military and police training. He continues to deny any involvement in Tara's disappearance.

"I don't wanna hurt any innocent civilian much less someone I spent five and a half years of my life with."

"What is clear is that there isn't a whole lot forthcoming about Tara's personal life to draw the conclusions we need to about who is the most probable suspect," Orange said. "Like in the Natalee Holloway case, the sexual activity of the woman in question is kept hidden. If her background reveals that she was a promiscuous woman, there will e less sympathy and urgency to solve the crime. That is one of the more striking aspects of the case, aside from Tara's vanishing, is the cover-up of Tara's personal life in order to protect her reputation."

UNSOLVABLE CASE?

Tara Grinstead's case is still being investigated. The GBI reports that they receive numerous leads per day, most of which are false.

Her body has never been found but her impact on the lives of those around her and her students will never be forgotten.

"I'm so sorry to hear about what happened to Miss Grinstead," said Christine Kang, a South Korean exchange student from Grinstead's class. "She is so caring and giving to her students. I am sure she will come home soon safely. I will pray for her every night."

JOANNA DENNEHY

124

When you take a closer look at the list of the bloodiest and most violent murders throughout the history, the chances are you will mostly encounter male names. Female serial killers are incredibly rare in our society. Women are unlikely to go out on a random killing spree and injure more than one person in a cruel way. When women do kill, they prefer using poison and their motives are very personal and driven by passion. Of course, there are always exceptions to the rule like Aileen Wuornos who became the most famous female serial killer. She shot and killed seven men in Florida over the course of several years.

You can only imagine the shock that spread through Peterborough, a small town in the eastern part of England when bodies started showing up in ditches over the course of several days. The investigators discovered that three grisly murders were committed by Joanna Dennehy. She was troubled but her life to that point only involved drugs and alcohol, at least to those who didn't know her well. Something happened and she simply snapped, going on a killing spree that frightened the entire Cambridgeshire, as well as the rest of the Great Britain. Her erratic behavior that escalated during those two weeks while she was on a prowl continues to puzzle experts and the law enforcement to this day.

Joanna's early life

Joanna Dennehy grew up in a middle-class family with a sister. Both parents were employed and they did their best to provide everything for the girls. Joanna's mother worked as a shopkeeper while her father was a security guard. She was very close to her sister Maria who is only two years younger than her. The age difference was insignificant and those two would spend all of their free time together, either singing or playing in the backyard.

However, everything changed once Joanna entered puberty. She began to rebel against her parents and her grades were on a steady decline. She would often come to classes visibly intoxicated. Joanna would run away from her home a couple of times, often with older boys. It seemed like her future will not be so bright. In 1997, when Joanna was only fifteen years old, she met her future husband in a park. His name is John Treanor and he was walking his German shepherd. He would later say: "She approached me. She had a thing for dogs – it just went from there. She'd fallen out with her parents and she was a bit of a free spirit but I liked her – in fact I loved her."

The two fell in love instantly, ignoring the age gap of six years. You can imagine that Joanna's parents weren't too thrilled about their relationship and they refused to allow Treanor to move in with the family. As a matter of fact, Joanna's parents kicked her out of their home in hopes she would leave Treanor and come back without him. But the pair was inseparable and they wanted to give their relationship a real chance. They found a house in Luton and lived with a couple of roommates in a very small place. Joanna continued to drink heavily while Treanor used marijuana. They would often steal food from shops in order to survive because they couldn't find a real job.

Joanna Dennehy was only seventeen when she gave birth to the pair's first child. Treanor was thrilled with this new addition to their small family and he got a steady job as a security guard, bringing the income to the household. However, Joanna wasn't too thrilled and she moved on to using cocaine after the baby was born. John said that Joanna became unstable in that period and would cheat on him with both men and women.

John left her and moved to Norfolk with their daughter but the pair would reunite once again soon after. Treanor just couldn't cut her off from her daughter's life. Joanna came to Norfolk and found a job as well. She was set on making a change and turning a new page in her life. That episode didn't last for a very long time and Joanna started drinking again. She even physically attacked John and almost hurt her then three years old daughter. John kicked her out of the house and Joanna started seeing a psychiatrist for a short time. She stayed away from her little family for a year and a half. Little is known about her life during that period but she was involved in prostitution and spent some time in prison as well. However, John took her back once again in 2003 despite her heavy alcohol use.

The pair welcomed their second daughter in 2006 and Joanna did her best to stay healthy this time around. But John noticed that she started abusing alcohol and drugs once again. She was very cold to her children and it seemed like she had no emotional connection to either of her daughters. She met a woman called Charmaine and two of them started an odd relationship that included sadomasochism. Joanna did have a history of self-injury but it intensified while she was with Charmaine. Her wounds were becoming more visible and Joanna did nothing to hide the scars from her family. She would cut herself all over her body, including the neck and arm area. A homemade face tattoo appeared on her face as well while she was dating Charmaine.

John moved out in 2009 after realizing that Joanna will not change anytime soon and that their children needed a safe environment to grow up in. She became more violent toward him and even threatened John with a knife. She would often attack her husband when she was drunk but the fact that she pulled a weapon on him clearly was too much. It was obvious that she didn't want to live a standard domestic life and that the girl John fell in love with was long gone. Joanna was mentally ill and her disorders were becoming more severe due to the alcohol and drug use. It was only a matter of time when she would go over the edge, either hurting herself or someone else. Joanna remained in the East of England, moving from town to town and trying to settle down somewhere.

Peterborough ditch murders

Joanna continued to lead a hectic life and she was given a twelve months sentence for an assault one year prior the murders. She stayed in a psychiatric hospital in Peterborough during that time as well. She was evaluated by a psychiatrist who discovered Joanna clearly suffers from depression. She was also diagnosed with an anti-social disorder and it was obvious she had a tendency to self-mutilate her body. When she was released from her hospital stay, Joanna had nowhere to go. She ended up moving in a small bedsit in Peterborough. The owner of the agency that rented her the bedsit, Kevin Lee, sympathized with Joanna and decided to help her out by letting her do some work for him. He had no idea that he would become one of her victims in a matter of months.

Joanna Dennehy's killing spree began on 19th of March 2013 when she stabbed Lukasz Slaboszewski straight through his heart. Slaboszewski arrived in the Great Britain back in the 2000s from Poland in hopes of finding better work opportunities. However, he began hanging out with the wrong crowd and abusing drugs. He was in the process of recovery at the time of his murder. Slaboszewski and Dennehy met for the first time only one day before the murder. He was certain that the two of them are an item and even mentioned to his friends that he had met an English girl. They made plans to get together the following day.

Dennehy invited Slaboszewski to her apartment and waited for his arrival. He was attacked within minutes and died right away after a single stabbing wound to his heart. It was Joanna's first murder and there was a lot of blood in her apartment. She was uncertain what to do about the body and knew that she needed help and made a decision to involve someone else in this crime by calling Gary Richards (also known as Gary Stretch) who was her boyfriend at the time. Stretch is a known petty thief who operated in the area of Peterborough for years but he was never involved in anything this serious. His towering stature made him stand out and Stretch was one of the tallest men in Britain at that time. He was obviously smitten with Joanna and covered her tracks by helping her dispose of the evidence.

Peterborough is surrounded by farms and fields so they selected a remote location east of the town. Stretch knew these villages and farms well so it was a clear choice for the dump site for Lukasz Slaboszewski's body. They left him in a drainage ditch and his corpse will not be discovered for weeks. After returning home, Dennehy felt ecstatic and thrilled after committing this crime. Her sadistic needs were met and she wanted the rush to last forever. Dennehy moves on to writing a list of her future victims and jolts down a total of nine names. She starts planning out her next murder right away.

Since no one has discovered Lukasz Slaboszewski's body for days now, Dennehy was certain that she had a complete control of the situation. She moves into another house owned by Kevin Lee who rented her a bedsit when she moved to Peterborough. The two have begun to see each other occasionally and Dennehy was regarded as Lee's lover. After the move, she meets John Chapman. He was a navy veteran who lived in the same housing complex and also was Dennehy's roommate. Two of them became somewhat friendly because Chapman was also addicted to alcohol. However, Dennehy turned on Chapman and threatened that she would say Kevin Lee about his excessive drinking. She wanted to get him kicked out of the housing and loved the control she had over him because of that. They had a third roommate Leslie Layton who would soon enough become Dennehy's second accomplice.

Joanna Dennehy moved quickly. The plan was to make John Chapman very drunk and Dennehy would enter his room and murder him. Ten days after the murder of Lukasz Slaboszewski, Layton and Stretch spent a day with Chapman and the two men left the shared housing after a couple of hours. They were drinking alcohol and talking. Once Chapman retreated to his room, Dennehy grabbed her switch knife and sneaked in. She jumped on unsuspecting Chapman and continues to stab him six times. It is clear that she is becoming more and more violent because this crime speaks of anger and fury she feels toward the man as well as the enjoyment of taking someone else's life. She was escalating in a way that is uncommon for a female killer. Dennehy would then call Gary Stretch and sing 'Oops I Did It Again' over the phone which is a proof of her bizarre behavior. The photos of Chapman's dead body will be found on Leslie Layton's phone and they would help the investigators determine the estimated time of death. Those photographs would also serve as evidence against Layton and his involvement in the murders.

Gary Stretch cleaned up the crime scene once again even though Dennehy didn't ask him directly to do so. It seems like Dennehy wasn't too concerned about people finding out while Stretch clearly understood the consequences of her actions. The investigators would later suspect that she choose Chapman as her next victim because he was 'an easy kill' for her due to his alcoholism and she felt the need to go through the process once again. It was also an urgency to continue her killing spree as soon as possible. The next name on her list was Kevin Lee, her landlord, and occasional lover. Dennehy didn't want to wait for days like before and needed to kill right away. So she made a call to Lee, inviting him over. He didn't suspect anything because they have met before in similar circumstances and Lee expected a sexual encounter between the two of them. He fell for Dennehy's charismatic personality and couldn't imagine that something sinister could happen to him. Unfortunately, he was very wrong.

Chapman's body was still in the house when Kevin Lee arrived. He knew that Joanna was unpredictable so when she asked him to put on a sequined black dress, he saw it as a harmless game. Once they start making out, Dennehy pulls out her knife and starts stabbing Lee. He had multiple wounds all over his body and this murder was done in a deranged frenzy. Dennehy calls Stretch and Layton once again and the trio drags Lee's body into his own car. Dennehy is oddly proud of murdering Lee and she wants his corpse to be found quicker. They leave him in a ditch but also position his body in a very humiliating pose. The sequined dress stayed on him.

They drive away and purchase gasoline in order to set fire to Lee's car. The trio is doing everything in order to cover up their tracks and destroy the evidence. They still had the body of John Chapman to get rid of. After they burned Lee's car, they returned to the housing unit and loaded Chapman into a vehicle. Three of them go straight to the place where Stretch and Dennehy left Slaboszewski's body. They lay two men next to each other and didn't even bother to clean up anything. None of them cared a lot about getting caught at this point.

On 30th of March 2013, a local farmer was going around doing his daily chores when he discovered a horrific sight. It was the body of Kevin Lee laying in a ditch. The police were called immediately and the team arrives straight from Peterborough. They identify the body right away but they are unable to find substantial physical evidence about the perpetrators of this crime. Since this is the area outside of the residential parts of Peterborough, there are no cameras that could have captured the criminal who committed this murder. They are shocked at the ferocity and the number of stab wounds he has on his body. The law enforcement was certain that a male killer was behind this.

Joanna wanted to kill again but she knew that doing that in Peterborough would be very dangerous. She suspected that the police are already looking for Kevin Lee. After all, he was a family man and his wife and children are probably worried for him. Joanna makes a decision to drive to another town with Stretch. They were both fleeing Peterborough as well as planning to find new targets.

The law enforcement starts digging into Lee's life and relationships. White Lee's wife is oblivious to his affair with Dennehy, his friends do tell the police about her. They soon discover that Joanna Dennehy is friends with some shady characters, namely Gary Stretch. Since he already has a history of criminal behavior, they assumed he was their prime suspect while Joanna might be the link to Kevin Lee and also his unwilling accomplice. After all, Gary Stretch is extremely tall and bulky so he could have overpowered Lee easily. They cannot locate either of them so it is clear that the pair is on the run from the police.

The madness in Hereford

Dennehy and Stretch make a quick stop at a gas station and they rob it. They are caught on the surveillance cameras and the police who already linked Stretch and Dennehy to the murder of Kevin Lee are closing in on their location. The couple arrives at Hereford which is a town located west of Peterborough. Dennehy needed to find her next victim so they cruised the streets of Hereford in hopes of finding a target. Joanna's mental state was completely out of control and Stretch would later tell the police that she said: "I want my fun. I need you to get my fun."

They noticed a man walking a dog and they drove up to him. The man's name is Robin Bereza and he is sixty-four years old at that time. Dennehy jumps out of the vehicle with her knife and attacks the man. She repeats her modus operandi and stabs Bereza ferociously then leaves him to die on the street. There were plenty of witnesses around and the police were contacted immediately. The pair drives away and locks in on another victim very quickly. John Rogers was also walking a dog and Dennehy did the exact same thing – scaring the fifty-six years old man by jumping out of the car and launching herself on top of him. He was easily overpowered and Dennehy wounded him badly. Luckily, both Bereza and Rogers did survive these attacks because the police and the emergency acted swiftly.

Hereford police issued a warrant and they were on a lookout for the vehicle that was described by the eye-witnesses. Soon enough they get a tip about the car and a patrol is dispatched there. The police officers discover Dennehy sitting on a passenger seat. Stretch was nowhere to be found. She was completely covered in blood and held a knife in her hands. However, Joanna remained composed and calm. She didn't make any attempts to get away or run from the police. They transported her to the police station and started the interview about the involvement with the murder of Kevin Lee, as well as the random attacks on residents of Hereford. Police caught up with Gary Stretch outside of Hereford and he was escorted to the same station. The police started questioning him but they soon realized that Stretch was just an accomplice. He knew how interrogations worked and he didn't provide the police with any extra information. However, the detectives noticed that Gary Stretch simply wasn't too clever to go on a killing spree for weeks and avoid the authorities. They came to a conclusion that their prime suspect is sitting in the adjacent room and as odd as it seemed at that time, the murderer was a woman. It was evident that this was an unusual crime that will become even more grisly after the discovery of Chapman and Slaboszewski.

Less than twenty-four hours after the arrest, another farmer discovered two corpses in a ditch outside Peterborough. The law enforcement arrived at the scene and they noticed the similarities between these two bodies and the murder of Kevin Lee. The wounds were almost identical and the fact that they were left in a remote drainage ditch suggested that the three murders are linked. As soon as they identified the victims, they made a connection to Dennehy. It was obvious that they had one of the rarest killers on their hands and luckily, she was caught and couldn't do harm to anyone else.

The examination and the trial

Joanna Dennehy is a unique murderer because a female killer rarely shows open acts of violence toward her victims. During the police interrogation, Dennehy clearly stated that she didn't want to murder women. However, the list which was found in her room said otherwise. The fourth name is of a woman who lived with Gary Stretch at the time. The motives shocked the investigators because Dennehy said her only goal was entertainment. The psychiatric evaluation would discover that Dennehy suffers from borderline personality as well as psychopathic disorder and that she feels the need to always be in control. She enjoyed hurting other people and being the one in charge. She didn't feel any remorse for her actions.

When there is a team of killers consisting of a male and female, the man is usually the one who gives orders. So when the detectives discovered that there was a second accomplice involved in the crime, they were baffled. Joanna appeared in front of a judge in November of 2013. The public expected that she would plead not guilty. She once again shocked everyone by admitting her involvement in the murders. It was a way to keep everyone interested and on their toes. Joanna loved the attention and being in the public eye.

Both Gary Stretch and Leslie Layton were charged with helping Joanna during her killing spree. They weren't called as witnesses during Joanna's trial. Two of them appeared in court in February of 2014 and were found guilty. Gary Richards also known as Stretch got a harsher punishment and was sentenced to nineteen years behind the bars with the possibility of release. On the other hand, Leslie Layton got fourteen years for covering up the evidence and not informing the authorities of the crimes that were taking place in his place of residence.

Joanna's court date was on 24th of February 2014 and she was sentenced to life in prison without the possibility of the parole. After the psychological assessment, it was obvious that Dennehy cannot be rehabilitated. Her mental disorders are too severe and she lacks the empathy and emotions towards other people. Her younger sister Maria wasn't too surprised with the judge's decision. She would later say: "I think the people, the drugs and the environment she went into triggered something dark inside her." Joanna joined the ranks of the most notorious female killers in the Great Britain because there were only two similar punishments in the history of this country – Myra Hindley who assisted Ian Brady with the infamous moor murders and Rosemary West.

Escape plan

Before she was scheduled to appear in court for her final sentencing, Joanna Dennehy started planning her escape from prison. She wrote down every last detail in her diary which was found by the guards who were shocked by the contents. Since the prison featured biometric locks, Dennehy wanted to grab one of the guards and cut off their finger in order to get through the security checks using their fingerprints. It was unclear if she wanted to murder a guard or injure them. Due to this event, Joanna was placed in the solitary confinement even before the trial itself and remained there until the autumn of 2015.

She would later contact the High Court and say that her human rights were being violated by keeping her in the solitary confinement for a long stretch of time. Dennehy told the judges she was becoming even more depressed in isolation which led to severe self-harm episodes. The High Court dismissed these claims and went public by saying that everything was done according to the law and that the punishment was justified for plotting an escape.

Aftermath

The police investigators were under the media and public scrutiny after it was revealed that Joanna Dennehy was allegedly surveilled because she owned a dangerous dog at that time and kept it in the bedsit. It seemed like she was capable of passing by the unsuspecting police officers without any troubles. The people wondered if there was something that could have been done in order to prevent these murders.

Joanna is currently in Bronzefield Prison located in Surrey. She is not in solitary confinement but still locked away from other inmates. Dennehy is still fighting for her rights that were allegedly violated after the guards discovered her diary as well as the fact that she is still segregated from the rest of the prison population. Sources from Bronzefield Prison claim that she enjoys watching reality shows, especially those that include food preparation and that Joanna is working on her own cooking skills.

Regardless of her current interests and how normal Joanna might appear, it is safe to say that the combination of the mental disorders she suffers from is deadly to anyone who gets close to her. She will probably never be fit to rejoin the society so the fact that Joanna is behind the bars is a relief to many.

COLD BLOODED KILLER CHRISTINA WALTERS

137

JENNIFER MARTIN

Christina "Shea" Walters: Cold Blooded Killer or Victim of Circumstance?

The Crime

It was a typical, hot August North Carolina night on August 17, 1998. Eighteen-year-old Tracy Lambert and her twenty-one-year-old friend, Susan Moore, were planning a night out on the town. The two vibrant, young blondes did their hair and make-up together and made plans to meet with friends. They got into Moore's car, and headed out toward their meeting place.

Suddenly, they were being tailed by an angry group of young strangers. The strangers were waving guns out the window, flashing their headlights, and yelling. Moore attempted to flee the group, but in a moment of terrified disorientation, she pulled down a dead-end road. Three young men approached the vehicle with guns drawn and forced the women into the trunk of Moore's car. The vehicle began moving with one of the young men behind the steering wheel. When it stopped, the men opened the trunk and demanded the women hand over their jewelry. Once all the jewelry was taken from the women, the trunk was again closed and the car began moving once again.

The second time the car stopped, the trunk was opened to reveal a larger group against the back drop of a trailer park. The group began discussing how to "dispose" of the women, causing Lambert to cry out and plead for mercy. A young American Indian woman expressed disgust with Lambert's "pathetic whimpering," and slammed the trunk door back shut. The men piled back into Moore's car while the rest of the group got into a second vehicle. The cars followed one another into an open, rural area where Lambert and Moore were forced out of the car. Each of the women was dragged into the open by one of the men who had committed the carjacking. Moore began pleading for their lives. She reportedly asked the men, "What are you going to do to us? Are you going to kill us?" She followed the question by trying to compromise, stating, "We don't know what you look like. Just let us go." At that point, one man held a gun to Tracy Lambert's head and said, "Well, I'm about to open this bitch's third eye." Lambert then started crying and said, "Oh, my god, Susan. We're going to die. We're going to die. I don't want to die." The gunman then told Tracy to "Shut up" before shooting her in the head. Another man was holding onto Moore with a knife to her throat as she watched her friend be killed. She began sobbing and begged him not to cut her throat, offering to him that he could just shoot her, instead. He showed mercy in that one small instance and borrowed the gun from his friend, ending her life instantly.

By midnight, friends and family were already concerned that the women had not arrived at the social gathering and began to look. An anonymous phone call alerted the police that the caller had "seen some people get shot." Sometime around dawn, the bodies were reported as discovered.

Earlier that same night, Debra Cheeseborough was leaving work at Bojangles when a young man, his face hidden beneath a bandana, approached her, placed a gun to her side, and told her if she'd cooperate, he would not hurt her. He ordered her into the trunk of her own car, where she lay still, quietly praying as a group of young people, all unidentifiable beneath their bandana masks, climbed into her car and began driving. Presumably as they dug through the contents of her purse and glove box, one of the young men came to the realization that he had gone to school with Debra's daughter.

Debra felt a glimmer of hope in that instant. She thought that, maybe, because they had made a connection, they would let her go without harming her. That hope was crushed when she heard the young people joking about how they had disliked her daughter and how much fun it was going to be to get rid of her mother.

The group pulled the car into an isolated area of Fort Bragg and ordered Debra from the trunk. She cried and pleaded for her life to no avail. Several of the young people, each with their own gun, began firing bullets into her. She was shot all over her body until the group was confident that she was dead. They left her lying on the ground and drove away in her car.

Debra later testified that, as she laid in the field, she could hear the voice of her deceased mother comforting her. "She told me it wasn't my time yet," she said under oath. "She told me she was going to help me get to the road, but not too close where someone could hit me." Debra did manage to drag herself to the roadside, where she was spotted by a passing motorist. She survived her injuries that night and went on to testify against her attackers in court, ultimately putting many of them away for life.

The night of August 17, 1998 was, no doubt, life altering for all parties involved in the events that unfolded in Fayetteville, North Carolina. This included twenty-year-old Christina "Shea" Walter. On the night of the crime spree, Christina had gathered at her trailer home at 1386

Davis Street in Fayetteville along with friends Francisco Tirado, Eric Queen, John Juarbe, Tameika Douglas, Ione Black, Carlos Nevills, Darryl Tucker, and Carlos Frink. Having grown up on the "wrong side of the tracks," all nine of the young people who gathered at the trailer had aligned themselves with the "Crip" gang, although they each claimed different "sets" or subgroups of the gang. The subgroups had come together and realized that the gang, as a whole, was in need of money. They formulated a plan to steal a car and drive it through the front window of a pawn shop, where they would steal the inventory.

Earlier in the afternoon, the nine friends had gone to Wal-Mart. They bought bullets with which they were going to carry out their plan and stole clothing and toiletries. When they arrived back at the trailer, Tirado borrowed Christina's blue fingernail polish to color the tips of the bullets blue. This was symbolic, the group agreed, of the "Crips" gang.

After discussing their plan, the group split up. Christina, Douglas, Nevills, and Black called a friend to drive them into a quiet neighborhood. Christina gave Nevills a gun and told him to find a victim and put them in the trunk of a car, then return to her trailer within an hour and a half.

Debra Cheeseborough was their first victim.

After the group thought they had killed Cheeseborough, they returned to Christina's trailer where they discussed their plan further. They realized that they needed another car. Christina, Tucker, Black, and Queen took Cheeseborough's car in search of another victim, ultimately finding Tracy Lambert and Susan Moore.

After killing the two young women, the group decided to call it a night and meet up at the trailer the next day. However, Tirado had trouble sleeping and kept one ear to the police scanner all night. At around dawn, he called Christina and reported to her that bodies had been found. From there, the entire group, with the exception of Black and Nevills, fled to Myrtle beach in Cheeseborough and Moore's cars, using her cell phone to place calls back to family and friends.

On Tuesday, August 18th, police in Myrtle Beach arrested Juarbe and Tucker and impounded Cheeseborough's car. The next day, they received an anonymous tip that Christina had rented a room at the Bona Villa motel in Myrtle Beach. They checked out the tip and found Moore's car in the parking lot. There, they apprehended Christina, Frink, Douglas, Queen, and Tirado. Soon, there was a media frenzy.

The Outcry

Throughout Fayetteville, the deaths of Lambert & Moore and the brutally savage attack on Debra Cheeseborough left the community enraged. The news that the crime spree was related to gang activity created a frenzy of individuals calling to "clean up the streets." News outlets flashed pictures of Moore and Lambert, two white, blonde haired, beautiful young ladies, but were less inclined to show images of Debra Cheeseborough, a middle-aged black woman. This, according to the defense, fed into a racial divide. Without knowing that Cheeseborough was a minority woman, herself, many within Fayetteville believed the violence was a hate crime against white people, instigated by a violent gang of minority youths. The fact that the attacks had been random was lost in the coverage and, soon, Fayetteville found itself in the throes of racial and economic divide.

The Woman

Not much is known about Christina's life before the events that unfolded that fateful night in 1998. Based on statements presented to her attorney, we can surmise that Christina's upbringing was less than ideal. She has made claims of being abused physically, emotionally, and sexually as a child. In one story, which would later come back to haunt her during trial, she spoke of cutting a man with a box cutter as he was trying to sexually abuse her.

As is the case with a lot of youths who feel displaced from their families and communities, Christina sought the embrace of whatever makeshift form of family she could find. In her case, she fell into a crowd of similarly dysfunctional minority youths who claimed membership to one of the largest street gangs in America: The Crips.

As Christina reached adulthood, she was able to secure her own place to live, which opened up a meeting ground for herself and fellow gang members to congregate in. Because her home was often the meeting point, she found herself in the position of leader and would often have to assert her dominance over other gang members who tried to challenge her. There is little doubt that the control Christina found within the gang was a welcome change from her helpless childhood. Christina no doubt realized that, in her newly given position, she could find safety in her power. She became a fearless leader of her group and was unafraid to assert herself with dominance or even threats of death.

Until that August night, though, Christina had never actually killed anyone. As would be explained in court by her co-defendants, to kill someone for the good of the gang is one of the highest honors the Crips had established at the time. The honor was memorialized with a teardrop tattoo on the face following a "confirmed kill."

Christina saw the carjacking plan as an opportunity to earn the highest honor she could for her gang, securing herself a position of leadership for life. To those of us who have grown up in more mild environments, it seems to be an act of selfishness and a fool's errand. To Christina, though, it would mean a lifetime of security from anyone that would ever attempt to cause her pain.

As the gang made plans to secure funds for their needs, Christina made plans of her own.

As the events unfolded, Christina remained mostly quiet about her intent to kill the carjacking victims. As each of the cars were stolen, the women were brought back to Christina's trailer to discuss their fates. It was only then that Christina expressed her desire for the women to be killed.

To refuse to kill someone for the benefit of the gang would have been suicide. With no other option but to help Christina, the co-defendants carried out Christina's plan alongside her. Because they had done so, Christina was responsible for helping them attempt to escape punishment, which is why she paid the way for everyone to go to Myrtle Beach.

Some of Christina's supporters today make a case that Christina wasn't cold-blooded. She was simply living the only life she knew how to survive in, and that her case was unnecessarily worsened by the media attention and dishonesty of news outlets at the time. Rumors regarding Christina's character and the lifestyle of the gang itself began to circulate. Soon enough, the story had evolved into a tale that Christina forced the co-defendants to kill two white women as a form of initiation into the gang. This was simply not the truth, but it was a tale that the defense had trouble running from. In the end, Christina "Shea" Walters believed the rumors and unfair media exposure were responsible for the severity of her sentencing.

The Trial

Regardless of Christina's culpability, she suffered from having inadequate representation at her trial. She was advised that, because of the media attention surrounding the case, the courts would issue a change of venue and try her somewhere other than Fayetteville. Unbeknownst to her, she would have had to file a motion for the change of venue. By the time she realized the need for her to initiate the motion, it was too late to file and her case was stuck at the center of a media whirlwind.

Because of the public nature of the case, Christina believes she was unable to receive a fair trial. According to her defense, eight of the twelve jurors that were seated on the jury had already been informed of the details of her case by other potential jurors and courtroom staff prior to the trial beginning. The state of North Carolina rebutted this claim stating that each juror swore to be fair and impartial and to disregard any information they had heard or read prior to the beginning of the proceedings. The state also argues that Christina never objected to the jurors at the appropriate time when she should have. Christina argues that, again, her defense team failed her and she did not know her rights.

She also claims she did not know her rights when she failed to file a motion for the murders of Lambert and Moore to be tried separately from the attack on Cheeseborough. Trying the crimes at the same time, she says, is partly to blame for the outcome of the proceedings.

Probably one of Christina's most compelling arguments that she did not receive a fair trial, however, comes with evidence logged right into the court report, itself. During the selection of the jurors, the Judge actually left the court room. During that time, a reporter began interviewing a potential juror about the case. The transcript reads as follows;

Judge: And, Madam Clerk, would you go ahead and call another juror please for number five?

Clerk: Richard Council.

Judge: Thank you. Counsel, I have to make a phone call to my district attorney. If you'll give me just a moment, please? (Leaves courtroom)

(Number five, Mr. Council, enters court room.)

Bailiff: Sir, come on up and have a seat in number five.

(A male media representative was talking to the juror, Mr. Council, as the juror walked by.)

Court Reporter: Tell that guy to quit talking to the juror- that media guy.

(Bailiff, Sgt. David Farrell, directed number five, Mr. Council, in the box after Sgt. Farrell spoke to the media representative.)

(Judge returns to courtroom.)

Judge: Remain seated.

Bailiff: Come to order. Court's in session.

Christina argues that, because the media had time to address the juror, and because nobody in the court room bothered to inform the Judge of the interaction, the juror was tampered with prior to the beginning of the proceedings and had already been given an "insider's idea" of what the hope of the community was for the outcome of her case.

Finally, Christina says that her past was brought up in court unnecessarily, with facts "twisted" to make her seem like a more brutal and violent person than she really believes herself to be. This is where the case falls back to the instance of self- defense against a sexual predator. Again, the evidence is in the transcript:

Prosecutor: Did you say your dad almost killed a boy that you stabbed?

Christina: I haven't stabbed no boy.

Prosecutor: Did you say that?

Christina: No, ma'am. I don't remember saying anything like that.

Prosecutor: Do you remember saying the boy you stabbed was 20-something at the time?

Christina: Unless the person who wrote this was talking about when I had a boyfriend who was trying to take my shirt off and I sliced him with a box cutter, but that's not stabbing.

At this point in the trial, the Judge did excuse the jury momentarily to ask the prosecutor why they were asking these questions. During the conversation, the Judge asked the defense why he had not objected to the questioning, clearly recognizing that it was a bad direction for the defense to allow the questioning to go.

Failing Christina, yet again, the defense attorney responded, "Well, because we didn't care at the point she was at."

One has to wonder- if a judge sees a line of questioning that is so outrageous he will dismiss the jury and ask, himself, why nobody is objecting to it- how does the defense, itself, not recognize the issue? Christina's supporters say that she was being defended by a court-appointed attorney who, they claim, was already swayed by the media outcry against Christina. He did not wish for her to win her case, so he did not even try to offer her a solid defense.

During the same testimony, Christina admitted that she shot several .32 caliber bullets into Cheeseborough, only stopping once she thought the victim was dead. Cheeseborough was able to testify against Walters, although she stated in her testimony that she could not positively identify her shooters. In appeals, Christina has stated that she was not well- advised by her attorney and only confessed to attempting to kill Cheeseborough because she believed that, because the victim of her shooting had survived, she would not be tied to the deaths of the other two women.

His failure to object to the unfair questioning, compiled with his failure to alert the judge of the jury tampering and not clearly outlining Christina's rights to her prior to trial are all signs indicating that, perhaps, Christina and her followers may be correct in their assumption.

In July of 2000, the trial came to a close with Christina Walters sentenced to Death. Eric Queen and Paco Tirado were both also sentenced to death in the months prior. With the ruling, Christina became the fifth woman on North Carolina's death row and secured herself a place as one of the state's most notorious female killers.

While there is little doubt that the acts committed against Tracy Lambert, Susan Moore, and Debra Cheeseborough on that August night were horrendous and cruel, there is reason to question whether or not Walters received a fair trial and sentencing in accordance with her legal rights under Federal law. Around the country, as news of the court case spread, Walters acquired supporters who felt empathy for her unfortunate upbringing and believed that she had been "railroaded" in court. As her following grew, the case began receiving attention from a new light, ultimately leading to a re-examination of the facts.

The Commuted Sentence

In December of 2012, a North Carolina judge commuted Christina Walters's death sentence along with the death sentences of two other convicted killers as part of the scaling back of the Racial Justice Act. The decision in each of the three cases came after a four-week deliberation on their individual cases in which the prosecution was proven to have made a conscious and indisputable error to reduce the number of black jurors in the original trials.

Although each of the prosecutors argued that they had, in fact, not made any such effort, the judge said that it was ultimately their own mannerisms and testimony that proved otherwise. "The conclusion is based primarily on the words and deeds of prosecutors involved in these cases," he said. "Despite presentations to the contrary, their words, their deeds, speak volumes. During presentation of evidence, the court finds powerful and persuasive evidence of racial consciousness, race-based decision making in the writings of prosecutors long buried in the case files and brought to light for the first time during this hearing."

Christina Walters, a Lumbee Indian, having been proven to have been tried unfairly based on her race, was commuted from death row to a life sentence without the possibility of parole.

The Repeal

In December of 2015, the Supreme Court vacated the commute claiming that the Judge did not give prosecutors adequate time to respond to a statistical study on race in the North Carolina state court system. The Racial Justice Act was also overturned, causing Christina Walters to, once again, have to appeal her case.

The study referenced concluded in 2011 showed that racial bias played a role in culling jurors before death penalty trials. Prosecutors disagreed with the claims, stating that the race of the juror doesn't play a role in their decision for keeping or releasing someone from the jury selection panel. The study examined 173 capital trials over a 20-year period to accumulate evidence to the contrary.

Qualified black jurors were over twice as likely to be released from panels under peremptory strikes according to Michigan State University's study of capital cases ranging from 1990 to 2010. Prosecutors argued that the study was invalid because the range of statistics stretched out far too broadly, failing to present an accurate depiction of how jurors are currently selected.

The Supreme Court encouraged both sides to prevent additional studies to support their claims.

In January of 2017, Christina Walters's legal team appealed her death sentence by using the now-repealed Racial Justice Act. Prosecutors argued that she couldn't use the repealed act because it has been repealed. Her defense argued that she had obtained relief under the Act and that it was unfair to strip her of that relief retroactively.

Judge Spainhour from Raleigh, North Carola presided over the case. He decided that Christina Walters's case was still pending under the Racial Justice Act and, therefore she could no longer use the repealed act.

There is little doubt that Christina Walters and her supporters will continue to appeal their case in pursuit of a commuted sentence or a retrial. With the buzz surrounding the case, it's hard not to look at the entirety of the situation objectively to determine if Christina is really the cold and calculated killer that prosecution in the original trial portrayed her to be or if, instead, she is a young woman led astray by circumstance, then railroaded by a court system designed to work against her.

Jay Ferguson, an attorney on her legal team, was quoted in the Fayetteville News Observer as saying, "We are confident that, no matter how many hearings are held or studies completed, we will win this case. The evidence of racial bias in jury selection is simply overwhelming and undeniable. All this decision will do is add more delays and cost the state millions to conduct new studies and hold new hearings. We will be throwing more taxpayer money into a hopelessly broken death penalty."

UGLY AS HELL: The True Story of Serial Killer Martha Wise

CARLA GLENN

"The Devil made me do it," she said. "He came to me in my kitchen when I baked my bread and he said, 'Do it!' He came to me when I walked the fields in the cold days and nights and said, 'Do it!' Everywhere I turned I saw him grinning and pointing and talking. I couldn't eat. I couldn't sleep. I could only talk and listen to the devil. Then I did it!" - **Martha Wise**

Martha Wise was born in Hardscrabble, Ohio to parents who were farmers.

Her life fit the name of the town she was from, as she had to endure a harsh life of manual labor and insults from childhood up until her death.

When she entered school, her teachers immediately labeled her as "dull" and "stupid."

"She was the dumbest kid there," one of her teachers said while another recalled that Martha was "the dullest child in school. She was even too dull to make trouble."

Throughout Martha's childhood, she never met anyone who greeted her with kindness in the tough luck town of Hardscrabble. One of her classmates remembered Martha as "always crying and every time anyone spoke to her she would burst into tears."

With no friends or teachers on her side, Martha created her own little world of imaginary friends. She would have numerous playmates that were invisible only to her and have animated conversations with them.

Labeled "feeble minded" by her educators and a "moron" by the even less sympathetic neighbors, Martha's own parents held little hope for her future.

"A deep sense of self-pity, not at all unwarranted, grew in Martha," wrote Tom Sellers. "Just as she poisoned those who laughed. She learned to see the devil in every leering face she met."

Martha had three brothers and a sister but her family had little faith in her ability to leave the homestead and get married. Martha had deep set eyes that were spread wide across her face. Her putty nose, thin lips and broad cheekbones did little to flutter the hearts of eligible suitors.

"Let's face it," her own mother said to her sister Lillie. "Martha is ugly. Damn ugly."

In 1906, however, Martha would meet a man named Albert Wise at a box social. These box socials allowed eligible women to cook up a meal for bachelors in the area who would bid on their box. If they won the bid, they would be entitled to a date with the creator of the boxed meal.

"That was one helluva chicken sandwich," Albert Wise said as he chomped down on the meal that Martha had prepared for the box social. He was over twenty years her senior and not much to look at himself. Martha was in her early twenties but seemed destined for spinsterhood. She took to Albert's brief courtship all too willingly.

Albert would ask for Martha's hand in marriage and she happily obliged. He did not take the union seriously, however, as he didn't even give Martha a wedding ring.

"Let's go," Albert said after they exchanged vows. "There's work to be done."

Martha's dream of meeting and marrying Prince Charming soon came to a crashing halt as she arrived at Albert's fifty acre farm.

"Get to work bitch," Albert said as he threw a shovel at her. He then led Martha out to the pig sty where he forced her to clean up after the hogs.

Martha drew ridicule throughout the town of Hardscrabble as she was forced to do such harsh manual labor. The women in town worked hard but none of them were forced to slop the hogs.

Albert would work Martha like a rented mule. It became apparent that he married the homely young woman simply because he wanted a domestic slave.

"Hurry up!" Albert called out as Martha shoveled the pig feces into the compost pile. "After you're done, hoe the field and milk the cow. And then get your ass back inside and make me a chicken sandwich!"

Despite his advancing age and Martha's lack of appeal, Albert's sexual appetite was voracious. Martha would describe their sex life as "joyless" and "miserable." She would become pregnant but miscarry the baby because her farming duties were so strenuous. She and Albert would have four children, however; Everett, Gertrude, Kenneth and Lester.

Feeling nothing but self-pity, Martha developed an odd habit of attending funerals. She attended any funeral that was held in or near the town. She didn't care if she had known the deceased or not. When people asked what she was doing there she simply replied "I like funerals."

Martha's life on the farm continued to grow harsher as the money grew tight.

"Work, bitch, work!" Albert would cry out as he raked a hickory stick across Martha's buttocks and legs, imploring her to work harder around the farm. He would beat her as if she were a farm animal until one day Martha finally broke.

She would poison Albert in 1923 but would never be charged with the crime. The doctors performed no autopsy and chalked his death up to "stomach inflammation."

His death, however, had a silver lining for Martha as she was able to collect on his insurance policy. She obtained some freedom for the first time in her life and would often take long walks around the town, neglecting the farm work.

She also made sure that Albert had an elaborate funeral.

"There was music and there were flowers," Sellers wrote. "The children were clean and dressed in their best. And from nowhere, almost, there appeared the usual association of bearded ladies who hover about the homes where death has visited to offer consolation and solace. The stream of life suddenly lost some of its drabness."

Martha finally received some long sought after attention and sympathy during the funeral for her departed husband.

"I like funerals," she mumbled quietly to herself as the well-wishers slowly milled out of the graveyard.

Despite being free from the yoke of Albert, the now forty-year old Martha had four children to raise by herself. She continued indulging in her funeral fetish, attending services of strangers and making a spectacle of herself.

Martha would arrive at the funeral early and sit in the front row. She would cry and wail, screaming to the heavens, "Why! Why! Why!"

The theatrics would oftentimes scare other attendees while others would stare at Martha in open-mouthed shock.

"Dressed in her weeds, she attended all funerals within reach, her sobs and lamentations rising above the smothered tide of keening by the bereaved women," Sellers wrote. "Weeping became sheer joy to her. When the slightest thing went wrong she drew her children about her and sobbed, not the dry, choking sobs of the truly grief-stricken, but the free flood of tears that come easily to those afflicted with self-pity."

Despite being considered one of the ugliest and least desirable women in town, Martha decided to put herself back on the market for a new man.

Problem was that Martha was not a very attractive woman. She was now in her forties and had four young children. Friends and neighbors described her as a woman with a "pinched face and sunken eyes."

She would find a friend in Walter Johns, however, meeting the younger farmhand as he worked on a neighbor's property.

Martha would try her best to woo the man whenever she could. She would make him chicken sandwiches, bake fresh cookies and bring fresh lemonade to him on hot summer days when he worked out in the field. Johns was polite and appreciated the gestures but did not return the romantic interest.

Martha continued to try to win the man's heart through his stomach. Her actions soon brought ridicule from her neighbors and family members. They teased her mercilessly. Her own mother and aunt called her a "cradle snatcher" when they caught wind of the fact that she was trying to entice the younger man into an affair.

Both mother and aunt would take the bull by the horn and talk to Walter. They falsely accused Walter of having an affair with Martha which he vehemently denied. Disturbed by the accusations and rumors, Johns would move to Cleveland and would no longer see Martha.

Martha learned of his departure and was livid, blaming her family.

"Why can't you just let me have a little bit of happiness!" she cried out.

"You're old," her aunt said. "And ugly. It is for the best."

Martha, however, would begin to plot her revenge. The voices in her head, the ones from her childhood, being whispering louder in her ear.

"Do it," they wheezed.

"Do what?" she would ask aloud.

"Do it," the voices whispered again as she entered the drug store. She would purchase over fifty grams of arsenic which was supposed to be used only to kill rats.

"Do it," the voice in her head echoed, becoming louder.

Cradling the arsenic bottle, Martha knew what the voice in her head wanted her to do.

Martha would spike her family's kitchen water bucket with the rat poison. On Thanksgiving day of 1924, Martha would encourage all of the family members to drink up, excluding herself and her own children. Her mother Sophia, would fall ill as well as the rest of the visiting family.

"Arsenic poisoning is painful," Sellers wrote. "Imagine excruciating stomach pain for weeks on end. Your stomach is tied up in painful, tight knots and you can't stop vomiting and defecating."

Martha's mother, Sophia, would die after suffering for over three weeks. The rest of the family members would eventually recover.

Martha, however, would go all out for her mother's funeral, both in ceremony and performance.

"Why! Why! Why!" she wailed in the church pew as family members watched on in horror. She had to be helped in and out of her seat, her grief so severe.

She still had revenge on her mind, however. Her family had intervened and cost her the love of her life in Walter Johns.

They had to pay.

"Do it," the voice in her head repeated. "Do it."

Martha's face turned to stone as she knew her job was still incomplete. She still had a lot of left over arsenic remaining.

During the New Year's Eve celebration a few weeks after her mother's death, Martha once again spiked the family water bucket with arsenic.

This time, her uncle Fred and aunt Lillie Gienke were the victims along with their six children who ranged in age from nine to twenty-four.

Her aunt Lillie wold die on January 4th while the children and uncle Fred continued to have stomach cramps and uncontrolled bowel movements.

"It's bad," Fred said in describing his own violent battle with diarrhea. "Really bad."

The children would become hospitalized while Fred would lose his battle on February 8th, dying at the age of fifty-nine.

Their children were shipped off to neighbors and relatives. One of the children ended up in Martha's care.

Authorities, however, grew suspicious after the death of Uncle Fred. They initially thought the family were victims of botulism or other natural poisoning but that was not the case.

Sheriff Fred Roshon began looking into the activity of Martha and found out that she had purchased large quantities of arsenic at the local drug store. He decided to exhume the body of Martha's aunt Lillie and an autopsy revealed that she had, in fact, traces of arsenic in her stomach.

"But who could do this?" Roshon thought to himself. He brought in prosecutor Joseph Seymour and the two began to suspect Martha.

"Administration of the poison appears to have been accidental or the work of a moron," Seymour said to the press as they badgered him for answers on the rash of deaths.

Seymour would receive an anonymous letter in the mail, however. It read : "I just want to make a suggestion-see if you can find out if there was ill feeling between Martha Wise and Lillie Gienke. I know something of the treachery of this Martha Hasel Wise and also her craftiness to evade suspicion. She is what you might call a moron. Could it be to get rid of her mother and get the property and of Lillie of suspecting her. She claimed to have been made sick too, but that may be a lie too."

Seymour informed the Sheriff of the letter and the men brought in Martha for questioning.

"My heart bleeds for them (her dead family members)," Martha said as she entered the interrogation room. "It must have been a monster that would kill them, and my poor, innocent old mother, why did they kill her? It was terrible. I sometimes think they were poisoned by accident. Because I can't imagine anyone being so terrible."

Sheriff Roshon was joined in the room by his wife Ethel and Seymour.

"We know you did it, Martha," the Sheriff said, sitting across from her.

Martha said nothing. She gulped hard and looked at the Sheriff's wife for help.

"Why not confess and get it off your conscience?" Seymour said.

"You're wrong, Mr. Seymour," Martha said. "I would never a done such a thing."

"Why did you buy all of that arsenic?" Roshon asked.

"To kill some rats," Martha said, shifting in her seat.

"Rats?"

"Yeah."

"You purchased enough arsenic to kill all of the rats in the whole state! You did it to kill your family! Admit it!"

"No," Martha shook her head violently. Her eyes began to water.

"Martha, we found arsenic in your aunt Lily's stomach," the sheriff explained, holding up a receipt of her purchase of the rat poison. "We know how you warned your own kids not to drink water at grandma's or Uncle Fred's."

Tears streamed down Martha's face. Her bottom lip began to quiver.

The sheriff stared at the woman, letting several minutes pass. It began to rain outside.

Ethel Roshon, the sheriff's wife, then took Martha's hand.

"Listen, Martha," Ethel said. "Do you hear those raindrops? Do you hear what they're saying? They're saying: 'Drop-drip-drip. You-did-it. Drop-drip-drip. You-did-it.' You did it, Martha! You know you did! Listen to it, Martha. It's the voice of God. He's telling you to tell the truth!"

"Oh, my God!" Martha screamed. "Yes, I did it. I put arsenic in the water bucket. But it was the Devil that told me to. He came to me, laughing and grinning, while I baked my bread. He came to me when I was a-hoin' in the fields. He kept telling me to do it while he follered me in the meadow. It was the Devil done it."

"The devil?" the sheriff asked.

"They told me I had no business wantin' to get married again. Said I was old and ugly. They laughed at me when that young fellow threw me over. I hated them and the Devil said: 'Kill them!' And I did. I liked their funerals. I could get dressed up and see folks and talk to them. I didn't miss a funeral in twenty years. The only fun I ever had was after I kilt people."

The sheriff got up out of his seat, aghast. "Why, Martha? Why would you do such a thing?"

"I'm irresistibly attracted to attending funerals," Martha said. "We do not have enough funerals here. I had to create them myself. I'm sure you understand."

The trio sat in silence, letting the weight of the confession sink in.

"I did it all," Martha said. "I stole jewelry from friends. Family. The barns that burned down? That was me. I like fires. They were red and bright, and I loved to see the flames shooting up into the sky."

Sheriff Roshon never made the connection between Martha and the three churches that had been set on fire in the town. He now had his perpetrator that he would have never suspected.

The prosecution attorney met with doctors and they all determined that Martha was suffering from "mental dementia." Despite the diagnosis and facing pressure from both the newspaper and local townspeople, Seymour decided to prosecute Martha to the full extent of the law.

The trial was set for May 4th, 1925.

Wise would plead not guilty despite the fact that she confessed during the police interrogation.

The press and local townspeople had a field day with daily news reports and gossip. Martha would be described as the "Borgia of America," a reference to the crime family that specialized in arsenic poisoning.

The press had built her up as a monster, printing unflattering pictures of her and then describing her as a 'super-killer' when she went into the courtroom. One newspaper wrote "her face was drawn, her eyes downcast. There were lines about her eyes and mouth, testifying to the mental suffering thru which she has passed during the months that she has been in jail. Her hair was combed straight back from her wrinkled and yellow forehead. Her eyes were weird, dark caverns, deep-sunk behind her steel-rimmed glasses. When she was arrested her hair showed few traces of gray. Today it is thickly streaked with white...The woman walked like one very tired. Her shoulders sagged. Her head dropped on a sunken chest. Her clothes were clean, but ill-fitting over her gaunt form. Her hands hung listlessly at her sides, one clutching, claw-like, a small-blue handkerchief."

Martha was assigned an attorney named Joseph Pritchard who would prove to be just as moronic as Martha herself, a match made in hell. His initial argument to the grand jury was that Martha was insane and should not have to go to trial. The jury refused and Pritchard then had to come up with new ploys. He planned to foist the blame on Martha's sister-in-law, Edith.

Edith had been troubled by delusions that she was the one that had poisoned the Gienke and Hasel families. She became frightened that Pritchard would call her to the stand as voices in her head told her that she did it. When authorities informed her that Pritchard was going to force her to testify, Edith slashed her own throat with a paring knife. Martha's brother Fred then had a heart attack upon hearing of his wife's suicide. So instead of taking the stand to defend his sister, he was in the hospital.

Pritchard knew he was working against a stacked deck. Martha's own son Lester and three of Gienke's children would testify against the prosecution. Lester would inform the jury that his mother gave him distinct instructions not to drink the water during the Holiday parties.

Martha's nieces and nephews would hobble into the courtroom on crutches and struggle to take the stand. The prosecution made them describe their daily lives, giving detailed accounts on what it was now like to be partially paralyzed due to the arsenic poisoning administered by Martha.

Pritchard scratched his head for a new tactic. He convinced the authorities that Martha's love interest, Walter Johns, had put her up to killing the families as he was upset that he was forced to move to Cleveland.

Johns was then arrested and held in jail for a few days.

The press and local townspeople had a field day with the revelation. The townsfolk started rumors about Johns having an affair with Martha. They made jokes that the crazy Martha would be on all fours during their lovemaking sessions, barking like a dog as she experienced an orgasm.

Pritchard then called Martha to the stand and had her recount the time spent with Walter Johns.

"I would have carried this to the grave," Martha said. "I never intended to tell. But now that everybody is talking about it, I can't hold my tongue any longer. He never came to see me in the jail and at the trial he never looked at me, although he was there every day. Walter Johns told me to do it. It wasn't the devil-it was Walter Johns. They didn't want me to get married. He said to get Mother out of the way and I did. He made me do it! He put me up to it! He kept at me to do it! He told me I should get the arsenic and get rid of my mother, and then I'd be free and happy...I took my punishment. You scorned me. Now I tell."

"She lies," Johns said. "She lies. I don't know anything about this."

A police investigation would prove that Johns was an innocent man who was merely being nice to Martha. He was a married man with five children. A hard worker of whom no one had anything bad to say about.

"We were never lovers," Johns said, shaking his head after he was released from jail.

Pritchard was then forced to come up with something new in Martha's defense.

The man's name was Frank Metzger.

Pritchard had used this technique numerous times in his career. He would pay off a fake witness who would come forward and say what needed to be said in order to get his client off the hook.

"I call Frank Metzger to the stand," Pritchard said.

They watched as the small time criminal walked toward the stand.

"This man's story will save you," Pritchard whispered into Martha's ear.

"I know nothing of about the case," Metzger said as Pritchard began questioning him.

"What?"

"I never spoke to Mrs. Wise. I never saw Mrs. Wise. Ever."

Pritchard turned red. He had paid off Metzger but now the man reneged on his end of the bargain. The case was the talk of the whole country and Metzger sensed that there would be repercussions if he was caught perjuring himself.

Pritchard now had no choice but to allow the prosecution to question the man.

"The defense wanted me to perjure myself," Metzger said to a stunned jury. "I asked asked to have written out a statement that Martha Wise was, inside and that I saw her froth at the mouth and heard her bark like a dog. I never saw or heard any such thing."

Pritchard's trump card now coming to naught, he resorted to crocodile tears during his own closing arguments. He described Martha's wretched life in vivid detail and in closing focused on her mental illness.

"Pyromania, plus kleptomania, plus epilepsy, plus spinal meningitis equals insanity," Pritchard said as he returned to his seat.

"This is no town lunatic," prosecuting attorney Seymour said as he closed his own argument. "This is a cunning and sly murderer. Imagine her slipping into the Gienke home when no one was watching, pinching arsenic into their water pail, returning twice to add further poison-that's not the manner in which insane people kill. She bought enough arsenic to kill every one in the Hardscrabble district where she lived. She came to the Gienkes when they all were ill and told their doctor she thought their illness was influenza. That's not the act of an insane woman."

The jury would deliberate for less than an hour. Martha would be found guilty of first-degree murder but the jury suggested mercy in her sentencing.

The judge would sentence Martha to a life sentence under terms in which she could only be freed by executive clemency. At the time, it was highly doubtful that this clemency would ever occur.

"The devil made me do it," Martha said after her conviction. "Voices told me to. After I did it, it bothered me and worried me. I worried about it all the time. I feel better now...I feel better since I have told you all about it...It is the Lord's will that I should be punished and I know I must be."

Martha's children, Lester 14, Everett 11, Gertrude 10 and Kenneth, 7 were all placed into adopted homes. Martha's netw worth was worth only the eighteen-acre farm and $1800 in savings.

Martha would remain in the public eye, her crimes would become the stuff of legend in the Hardscrabble community. A news reporter would visit her in 1930, five years after her conviction.

Martha would express remorse in the interview and continue to describe encounters with the supernatural.

"I see ghosts," she said to the reporter. "Every night they come and sit on the edge of my bed in their grave clothes. They point their fingers at me."

Jail life would be a routine for Martha. She would take two baths a week. She would get up at 6 a.m. and have the lights turned off in her room by 8 p.m.

"I do what I am told to do," she said in describing her prison life. Her duties were similar to what she did on the farm. She fed the chickens and played with the rabbits. She found happiness in incarceration but would cry when reminded of her children.

She would be denied parole in 1946, 1951, and 1956 but finally got a break on December 26th, 1962.

After almost three decades in prison, Ohio Governor Michael DiSalle would commute Martha's sentence to second-degree murder. She would be paroled at age 79 but would have nowhere to go. Her family refused to take her in and the correctional institute could not find a rest home who would accept her. Initially, she was going to be placed in a rest home in Union county where the prison was located. She would fail the one-year residency requirement, however. Officials then made arrangements through a senior citizen center run by Murial Worthing.

Worthing had initially agreed to take in the elderly killer but reneged after discovering her personal history.

"No," Worthing said. "She cannot come into our house. I'm a food caterer. This is a small town. People would talk. What do you think would happen to my business? I'd even lose the job as a cook I'm now holding."

"After I did it, it bothered me and worried me," Martha said. "I worried about it all the time. I feel better now...I feel better since I have told you all about it...It is the Lord's will that I should be punished and I know I must be."

Martha's probation officer had no choice but to take her in for the night. The next morning, she drove her back to the jail as Martha wept.

"There was no reason why this woman should have ever left the reformatory," Governor DiSalle said after the plans for her to go to the Union county home fell through. "This casts a reflection on state workers up and down the line because somebody didn't do the job."

Her parole and commutation of her sentence was revoked simply because there was no where for her to go.

Martha was then forced to live her remaining years in the Marysville reformatory for women.

Martha Wise, the woman no one wanted, would die in prison on June 28th, 1971 at the age of 88.